RESCUE TUGS AT WAR

Rescue Tugs At War

A Personal Account Of Life In
The Royal Navy Rescue Tug Service

By Stanley Charles Butler RNVR

Edited by Peter Butler

YOUCAXTON PUBLICATIONS
OXFORD & SHREWSBURY

The original story was handwritten in 1979 and a spiral bound manuscript with title 'Not For Davy Jones's Locker' was produced in 2005.

This book was edited and produced by Peter P Butler.

Copyright © Peter Butler 2020

The Author asserts the moral right to
be identified as the author of this work.

ISBN 978-1-913425-50-0
Published by YouCaxton Publications 2020
YCBN: 01

All rights reserved. No part of this publication may be reproduced, stored in a retrieval system, or transmitted in any form or by any means, electronic, mechanical, photocopying, recording or otherwise, without the prior permission of the author.

This book is sold subject to the condition that it shall not, by way of trade or otherwise, be lent, resold, hired out or otherwise circulated without the author's prior consent in any form of binding or cover other than that in which it is published and without a similar condition including this condition being imposed on the subsequent purchaser.

YouCaxton Publications
www.youcaxton.co.uk

The book is dedicated to the memory of Stanley Butler's daughter Anne Foletti, who died suddenly of a heart attack in April 2005. Like her father, she died too young.

Many thanks to Clem Thompson for typing the original notes. Special thanks to my wonderful wife Anne Butler for her support and attention to detail during the long process of proof reading.

Contents

Chapter	Page
1 – Volunteers For Tugs	1
2 – The North Atlantic	14
3 – The Sinking Of The Rescue Tug *Englishman*	19
4 – The Glasgow Blitz And Travelling By Train In War Time Britain	23
5 – Enemy Activity At Sea Increases	27
6 – Iceland	33
7 – A Personal Tragedy	43
8 – The Coastguard Cutter *Alexander Hamilton*	45
9 – *HMS Sheffield* Hits A Mine	50
10 – A Stormy Night In Hvalfjordur – Rescuing the *El Illeo*	52
11 – Promotion And A Transfer To *HMRT Prudent*	57
12 – The Strange Story Of The *Lavington Court*	62
13 – More Rail Travel In War Time Britain	71
14 – Gibraltar, Freetown And Crossing The Equator	74
15 – South Africa And Our New Base – Durban	80
16 – Saving The *Sheaf Crown* And An Incident Of Looting	89
17 – The *Meliskerk* And The Disappearing Case Of Whisky	94
18 – Madagascar	101
19 – Salvaging *U-852*	103
20 – *U-852* And The *Peleus* Affair	105
21 – The Salvage Operation	112
22 – Honoured By The King	116
23 – The Trial	117
Epilogue	121

Appendix One—Ships That Stanley Butler
Served In Before Joining The Rescue Tug Service   125
Appendix Two—Assurance Class Tugs   127
Appendix Three—Letters Received   129
Appendix Four—Instructions For Search
Of German Submarine   132
Appendix Five—Report On U-boat (*U-852*)   136

Photographs:

Stanley Butler	11
Sub Lieutenant Walker	12
HMRT Restive	13
Sub Lieutenant Dusty Miller	56
Crew On HMRT Prudent	57
HMRT Prudent	58
Medals Awarded To Stanley Butler	116
Wedding of Stanley Butler and Patsy Kenny	123
Rivtow Lion	124

Introduction by the Editor

My father read many personal accounts of the Second World War, but never found one about the navy rescue tug service. To give these unsung heroes the recognition they deserved, he wanted to write an account of his own service on tugs.

Stanley Butler was a great story teller and had a very good memory for people and events. He hadn't kept a diary, so it was remarkable that he was able to recall such a detailed account of his life between 1940 and 1944. In those pre-internet days he spent many hours in the reference library.

Unfortunately he was unable to finish his story. On 1 June 1979 he died suddenly of a heart attack and his notes were put into a box and forgotten about. I discovered this box 25 years later and knew straight away that this valuable record had to be published. It gives a rare insight into the work of the rescue tug service, an account of his adventures on shore leave and details of his family life.

'Davy Jones's Locker' is where many seamen believe they go if they die at sea. My father was fortunate not to have been on a ship that was torpedoed, but a few times he was near to ships that were. Down in the engine room, the noise of a ship being torpedoed was incredibly loud. The vibration was so bad that it was as if the ship he was on had been hit. On one occasion, one of the engine room staff panicked and ran for the exit ladder. When asked where he was going, he said, "I'm not for Davy Jones". This is why I used the title 'Not For Davy Jones's Locker' for the spiral bound manuscript I produced and circulated in 2005. To help the current edition appear in online searches, I put the word 'tug' in the title. This explains why the book is now called 'Rescue Tugs At War'.

At the end of the book I've added an in-depth account of the last voyage of *U-852*, her salvage, and the trial of some of her crew. It is my attempt to finish a story my father was unable to finish.

Peter Butler – 2020.

1 – Volunteers For Tugs

WITHOUT A DOUBT, the evacuation of Dunkirk and the fall of France were a great shock to many people throughout the world. Those of us away at sea became worried about the possible invasion of England and the problems that could face other countries. Not long after leaving Canada, the commodore of our convoy received a message that we should return to Canada if England was invaded. Thankfully there was no invasion. By the time we arrived back in the UK, I had made up my mind to try and take a more active part in the war. At that time I was third engineer on the *S.S. Sithonia*, a large and very comfortable tramp steamer, and had just completed a second voyage to the gulf ports of the United States.

A representative of the Marine Engineers' Association called aboard the ship and mentioned that the Admiralty was requesting volunteers from the merchant service for service in rescue tugs. The word tug was very appealing at that time as it meant, or so I thought, being near home if the country was invaded. The appropriate application forms were attained, duly completed and posted off to the Admiralty. I then travelled down to Falmouth to join my wife and two sons.

My application was accepted and I attended an interview with Captain Roche R.N., the Base Engineer for Falmouth. At that time they were based in the Imperial Hotel near Falmouth station and dockyard. All went well and I was offered the position of 2nd engineer, which I accepted. During my interview with Captain Roche I asked what we were expected to do. He replied, "Save our ships. Remember that as your priority at all times. It is vital to the war effort to recover merchant and naval ships damaged by enemy action or other means".

Personnel joining the rescue tug section at this time signed on at the local shipping office as crew members of the First World War tug, *H.M.S. St Mellons*. This was purely a holding exercise. I signed up on 6 September 1940. My first job was working under the base engineer officer as a liaison officer between him and the dockyard.

In a small office on the dockside was Engineer Lt. Bath R.N., who was supported by three or four other personnel, who had all been recalled from retirement. At that time they were very busy with the many French ships of all sizes and shapes which had descended upon Falmouth after the fall of France.

On 21 September 1940, I was instructed to report "forthwith" to *His Majesty's Rescue Tug Champion* at Davenport dockyard. This was one of a number of French naval tugs requisitioned after their arrival from France. When I arrived aboard the ship it was around teatime on a Saturday afternoon. The only person aboard was the mate, or No.1, 'holding the fort' until Monday morning. The ship was in quite a mess from all the work being carried out by the dockyard. I was far from pleased, as I could quite easily have spent another couple of days with my family in Falmouth.

On Monday morning various members of the crew turned up, including the captain, chief engineer and 3rd engineer – names all forgotten now!

One incident at Davenport is worthy of mention. *Champion* was lying alongside a large floating dock, which was partly submerged alongside a quay near the Saltash Railway Bridge designed by Brunel. The floating dock was partly submerged because of air raids of an intermittent hit and run variety. Similar raids were taking place in Falmouth too. On the Wednesday after I joined *Champion* the day was pleasant with sunshine and broken cloud, and the skipper and I had gone ashore to chase some stores. The air raid sirens had been declaring 'warnings' and 'all clears' from early morning. Walking back to the ship the warning siren went off as we were crossing a parade ground. I mention this because we had a good view all round. Suddenly there was the sound of high-speed aircraft, and five German fighters appeared through a small heavy cloud, and levelled out to stay just under the cloud. A couple of seconds later two British fighters shot out of the cloud, just behind the Germans, diving fast. They must have spotted the enemy immediately, because up they went with enough speed to overtake. Before you could say "rescue tug", there were fighters all over the sky with guns blazing away. The whole lot disappeared in the general direction of France. What the outcome was, I never learned.

There was enemy aircraft activity on and off all day, but around 16.00 hours things really got going. I had been in the office of the floating dock to make a telephone call regarding stores. Upon returning to the deck of the floating dock, we saw that an elderly gentleman employed on the dock was looking up and over the Saltash Railway Bridge. Through the patches of blue sky, large numbers of aircraft were approaching in a V formation. As the sirens had not gone off, we thought they must be ours. We were soon disillusioned. When the first three aircraft were almost overhead, we saw small specks appearing out in front of them, rapidly getting larger and making the all too familiar noise of bombs. We threw ourselves flat on the deck, close to an electrical control box. One of the bombs fell on the quay alongside. Very soon sirens and anti-aircraft guns got going, and things became very hectic and noisy for about 45 minutes. In order to get some protection from our own bits of anti-aircraft shells returning to earth like a hailstorm, we got under one of the docks' mobile cranes. From here one got a good view all round of what was going on. Just over to my left was *H.M.S. Exeter*, having a major refit after her River Plate encounter with the German battleship *Graf Spee*. Ahead of us was the old *H.M.S. Victory*, at buoys out on the River Tamar. There were in fact ships of all types and sizes all around. Stuka dive bombers came on the scene at one stage and proceeded to dive bomb some oil storage tanks just beyond *Victory*. The first one came screaming down, let go its bomb and away up and off it went. The bomb exploded with the usual bright red and yellow flash followed by large quantities of yellow and black smoke. In this case I was surprised to see a complete tree rise up from the smoke, slowly turn over and over, and disappear back into the smoke. As a fan of air displays from the days of R.A.F. Hendon and the various air circuses touring the U.K., this daylight raid was really something. Unfortunately it was the deadly game of war and I believe 25 people were killed in Davenport, although little damage was done in the dockyard.

Within a day or so we went on a sea trial, and *HMRT Champion* was declared seaworthy. I can remember little of this ship, except that I didn't like the accommodation.

The mate and I shared a cabin just aft of the engine room. This was the only time in my sea-going career that I shared a cabin. We got terrible condensation from the deck head and found it difficult to keep dry or warm. Conditions in general were very cramped after a large and comfortable merchant ship. The mate and I discussed our lot in life, and took the view that we were volunteers and there was a war on, and the discomfort was part of our war effort. We consoled ourselves by discussing the lot of submarine crews, which was a lot worse than ours. After leaving Davenport we proceeded westerly and ran into some shocking weather. A merchant ship was in trouble somewhere south of Ireland. I remember the problems trying to get our towrope aboard in the bad weather and at night. Our captain was new like the rest of us, and also had his problems. The merchant ship still had crew members aboard, which was always a great help in handling the towing gear. We eventually got this ship in tow and headed for the Bristol Channel. During all this we had problems in the engine room. The main engine was triple expansion steam reciprocating and, rather unusually, all three piston rods had metallic packing. Usually the high-pressure cylinder had metallic packing and the medium and low-pressure cylinders had soft packing comprised mainly of asbestos. It is never advisable to attempt to tighten packing of any type when the engine is running. There are exceptions of course – this applies particularly to metallic packing. For some reason the old chief engineer got a 'bee in his bonnet' that we should tighten the low-pressure piston rod packing. We discussed it and I suggested we have a look at it when the present job was over. However he decided to have a go, 'behind my back', and we finished up with an extremely hot piston rod distorted with deep grooves. This brought on other problems. We did eventually reach a point off Barry where a harbour tug took over and we went to Cardiff for repairs.

At this stage my right knee was very painful and swollen as the result of slipping on the engine room plates in bad weather. Soon after arrival in Cardiff I found suitable digs and got in touch with my wife Kay, who soon arrived. The knee got to the stage that I had to get in touch with the naval base, where someone arranged for an R.N. doctor to visit me at my digs. The outcome was a spell in bed with suitable treatment. After about a week I was given sick leave and we returned to Falmouth. The journey to Falmouth took place on a Sunday via Bristol, where we had to change trains. We spent nearly 24 hours on Bristol station, because Newton Abbott station had been bombed during the night and the line was blocked. During our long wait we met up with a theatrical group in transit, which included Ralph Lynn. I can see him now taking a turn at amusing our very young son David in a very overcrowded waiting room. This was towards the end of September 1940.

After my spell of sick leave I was appointed once again to the base engineers' office and renewed my acquaintance with Engineer Captain Roche – this time to a desk in the corner of his office. He was a man I had the greatest respect for; very knowledgeable on marine engineering matters, and a naval officer and a gentleman to his finger tips. Discipline was 'by the book', so everyone knew exactly where they stood. But underneath it all he was a very humane and friendly person. He had retired sometime before the war and, like Eng. Lt. Bath and the many others in the dockyard, had returned to service on the outbreak of war.

During this spell at Falmouth I met Lt. E. Richards R.N.R. and Sub Lt. E. Phillips R.N.V.R., who had little to do, as they were awaiting appointments. Lt. Richards had been a merchant service chief engineer and came from Leith, Scotland, but was in fact a Welshman. He was very much the family man and visited my home many evenings in Falmouth. One funny little incident comes to mind when thinking of him. At the time in question, Falmouth was subject to 'hit and run' raids by enemy aircraft. Sometimes after dark an enemy aircraft would fly low round about Falmouth acting as a sort of decoy whilst another enemy aircraft was laying mines in Falmouth Bay and the harbour entrance. To help combat this situation, barrage balloons were in use over various parts of the town. Anti-aircraft guns were placed around the suburbs with sandbagged machine gun posts on various flat-topped buildings. On the night in question, Lt. Richards left our place around 22.00 hours to walk back to his accommodation. Whilst walking up a rather steep hill a German decoy aircraft appeared and decided to shoot down a barrage balloon. Lieutenant Richards, who was of rather portly build, had to run up the hill to avoid a fast falling blazing balloon intent upon his destruction, as he thought at the time!

Around the beginning of November 1940, Lt. Richards, myself and Sub Lt. Phillips were instructed to proceed to Hull to stand by a new tug called *Restive*, which was under construction. When we arrived, *Restive* was receiving engines and boiler in C.D. Holmes's fitting out basin, almost in the centre of Hull. I remember we were in 'digs' in Dover Street. Our landlady was extremely nice and looked after us very well indeed. She had unfortunately recently lost her husband at sea – he was a chief steward in the Merchant Navy.

There was always plenty to do getting a new ship ready for sea. *Restive's* sister ship *Prudent* had left just before, in mid November 1940. Unfortunately we were held up towards the end by incendiary bombs, dropped during one of Hull's many air raids. After some trials in the River Humber, we were declared ready for sea. This was a great relief, as we had had little sleep for about three days. Raising steam for the first time and testing equipment was a pretty continuous job, and went on day and night. On our third and final night in Hull, we had been invited to a dance at the town hall. I was never very interested in dancing, and, perhaps to my discredit, was inclined to support the bar. On this occasion there were new crew personnel to meet and chat with, and as is usual over a drink, we would talk about the ships we had served on, ports visited, and sort out the war in general and contemplate what our new ship could or could not do. I left reasonably early, and have only a vague memory of the walk back to ship, except that it was cold, even though I had my great coat on, and I was extremely tired. To cut a long story short, I woke up in the early hours stretched out on the quayside – not too far from the *Restive* – lying with my back towards the water. Had I turned over 'in bed,' I would have had a nice old drop of 20 or 30 feet into a very cold Humber! When I look back at this point, I think of it as the end of 'the honeymoon period' of my career in ocean tugs. The real business of getting to grips with the job had begun.

We sailed from Hull the next day, attaching ourselves to a small convoy going north. We were bound for Campbeltown, which we mistakenly imagined would be our base until the end of the war. Like all convoys, the top speed was that of the slowest ship. In addition to this, zigzagging put a few extra miles onto the journey. In actual fact this slow running on a new ship is not a bad thing at all, as it gives the main engine a chance to 'run in'. From the time we sailed we were having trouble with smoke from our oil burners. Believe me smoke is not popular with the people on the bridge in wartime. The last thing we wanted to do was draw attention to ourselves. But try as we might, we were unable to pinpoint our trouble to one particular watch.

We were sure that the incorrect setting of burners was causing the problem, but who was setting them incorrectly? The burners were changed each watch, so that a set prepared by the previous watch were put in use at the beginning of the new watch. These firemen would prepare a set for the next watch and so on. These burners are about two feet long and two and half inches in diameter. The front end, which enters the furnace, contains a set of nozzles. The back or outer end has connections for heated fuel oil under pressure and steam to atomise the oil as it is sprayed into the furnace. Preheated air is also fed to the furnace front by a steam driven fan. The air in question is preheated by the hot flue gases at the base of the funnel, by passing through tubes. When a set of burners has been removed, they are allowed to cool before the nozzle, in three parts, is taken to pieces. The nozzles vary in size, so that one with small jets would be used for low steaming requirements, such as lying in port with only an electric generator working and the odd steam pump. A burner with medium sized jets would be used for medium ship speeds. A call for full ahead plus would require the largest jets, with the force draught fan working 'flat out'. The burner nozzle sets are numbered so that a matching set of three parts would be used together.

Our problem turned out to be one fireman who could not read, so that the burners prepared by him were bringing discredit and the skipper's wrath on the wrong watch. However, all's well that ends well. I did my best to teach the lad in question to read and write. He was a nice lad, and like so many others he had been a bit backward at school and more or less left to fend for himself. He first went to sea in coal burning trawlers and this was his first experience with oil burning.

After passing through Pentland Firth, the convoy steamed in a northerly direction until dark and then swung southwest – much to everyone's surprise. That evening, after I came off watch at 20.00 hours, I went up to the bridge to hear the latest news and gossip, and have a general look round. Suddenly, about five miles or so astern, I saw a flare floating down on a parachute. Over the next twenty minutes or so, I saw more flares, which were appearing further away to the north all the time. From what I was told later, our convoy was observed from the air before dark and our original course reported. Just after this little episode, I was standing on the port side of the bridge when I happened to glance astern, and was shocked to see a small and completely blacked out vessel no more than 15 or so yards away from us. I went quickly and quietly into the wheelhouse, and reported it to the officer of the watch. By this time the bridge of the vessel concerned was just about level with ours. We heard a quiet voice through a megaphone asking if we were *Restive*, and the speaker identified himself as C.O. of a motor launch. He then passed on a message from the convoy commodore. This clandestine visit was because we were not allowed to use radio, and on this occasion, the use of a signal lamp was considered inadvisable. Our deck officers at that time were Lt. McFarlane R.N.R., Sub. Lt. Ted Noble R.N.R. and Sub. Lt. White R.N.V.R.

When we arrived at our destination, I was amazed at the beauty of Campbeltown and the surrounding Loch, and the Mull of Kintyre. To enter Campbeltown Loch from the sea or the mouth of the Clyde, we had to pass Davaar Island and then the small shipyard – both to starboard. Straight ahead across the loch was the small harbour with a jetty and quayside. It was originally built to handle commercial and fishing business. We were told that as early as 1498 coal was being mined in a small way three miles inland at Mill Dam. James Watt built a canal from there to Campbeltown to ship coal via coasters mainly to Northern Ireland. In 1877 a narrow gauge railway was built to handle this coal export business. Eventually the railway was extended to Machrihanish and carried both passengers and coal until closure in 1933. Another interesting point is that the Gulf Stream enables the gardens of Campbeltown to delight the eye with multi-coloured hydrangeas, azaleas and even palm trees.

In December 1940 Campbeltown was the only base for rescue tugs. When we arrived one or two rescue tugs were lying alongside the jetty, and a few more were at anchor along with a miscellany of other small craft. Alongside the east side of the jetty was a small submarine, which was part of the submarine training school. The Rescue Tug Section was building up a base in that area to receive and train lower deck personnel, under the direction of Lt. Robinson R.N.V.R. (later Lt. Commander). He was serving in *H.M. Rescue Tug Saucy* when she struck a mine in the Firth of Forth on 4th September 1940, and suffered leg and back injuries. Another *Saucy* was launched on 26th October 1942. The official title of the base was *H.M.S. Minora* and I believe a Commander E. G. Martin, C.B.E., V.R.D., R.N.V.R. was in charge. In Glasgow the Admiralty had taken over St Enochs Hotel and Rescue Tug Section had offices there under Commander Parker R.N.R. from Boston. As time went on, news trickled down to our level about what had been happening in the higher levels of Rescue Tug Section at the Admiralty in London. Rear Admiral Dewar had been called out of retirement to run the recreated Marine Salvage Department. He was assisted by Commander W. A. Doust as salvage adviser, who later became his deputy director. It was Commander Doust who sent out draft designs for ocean going rescue tugs, then desperately needed. Doust recommended that tugs should be of around 700 or 800 tons, of about 2000-horse power, and able to operate in the areas used by Atlantic convoys. They should also have sufficient fuel and stores to enable them to tow damaged vessels to safety, be fitted with the latest navigational and direction finding equipment and carry armaments. Salvage pumping and fire fighting capability was also stipulated. All rescue tugs were later fitted with two five-ton tanks of concentrated Foamite, which could be fed to the suction side of the large steam salvager and fire fighting pump located in the engine room.

Stanley Butler was second engineer on HMRT Restive from 1940 to 1942.

Sub. Lt. Walker was No. 1 on HMRT Restive.

HMRT Restive.

2 – The North Atlantic

OUR FIRST VISIT to Campbeltown was short and sweet. The one night we did get alongside enabled some of us to attend a social function laid on by local people. I met one family I can remember, the Langs. Mr Lang was retired but had been associated with the local shipyard. I mention this family in order to say thanks from all of us associated with rescue tugs to those many people in Campbeltown who went out of their way to be friendly and hospitable.

Restive went on station at Lough Foyle where the anchorage was just off Moville in the Republic of Ireland. We soon discovered it customary for the rescue tug personnel to go ashore there in 'civvies'. We found our way to Corrigan's Bar where, believe it or not, the cigarettes on sale were marked "H.M. Ships Only". These cigarettes seemed to be on sale in most of the shops too. There was in fact a great "changey for changey" business going on both there and in Londonderry. One item in great demand was silk stockings and such like for our womenfolk back home.

My memory of this period is rather vague. I can remember we left Lough Foyle and went out into the North Atlantic searching for a ship in very bad weather and after a couple of days nothing was found. A wireless message from H.Q. would have us chasing off to search for another ship in another area. By this time we were in mid-Atlantic, in weather you need to see to believe. Seasickness was quite a problem particularly with people new to the sea or from larger ships. In these early days in the North Atlantic I used to feel terrible for days on end, but was never actually ill. The most comfortable place to sleep was in the engine room store on the bales of cotton waste. More often than not it was impossible to eat in the wardroom, so people going on watch would make for the galley. My favourite diet under these circumstances was dry bread or 'dog biscuits' with a lump of cheese, and tea without sugar or condensed milk. In actual fact I was lucky because as time went on I overcame my seasickness and could eat and smoke under the worst conditions. Others were not so fortunate, and some even had to be taken off sea going assignments.

Tugs and other small vessels, including U-Boats, had to struggle through mountainous seas with gales whipping up spray. We would be pitched into the air by one towering wave, smacked down into the trough behind the wave, and then buried under tons of water by the next wave. Force ten gales were commonplace, with winds of 100 miles per hour or more. These conditions with spray and rain made it impossible to see much further than the next wave crest when you yourself were at the top of a wave. In winter, snow made conditions even worse.

On one of these occasions, we were carrying out a 'square' search. That is, when looking for a ship we would search the area around where the ship in distress was believed to be. The charts were marked with large squares divided into smaller squares. Allowances were made for the direction the ship could have been drifting in. The rescue tug would then proceed back and forth until the complete area had been covered. On the day in question I was on the starboard side of the bridge. I was there partly out of interest and with a desire to help when an extra pair of eyes might be useful. It was always a welcome change after a few hours in the engine room, where you are shut away from all the real interest and excitement. We were in fairly rough weather with wind and rain. Over to my right I saw, just for a fraction of a second, the deck work and funnel of a merchant ship. By the time I attracted the attention of the officer-of-the-watch, the ship had disappeared. Suggestions were made that I was seeing things. However, we changed course to our starboard and shortly saw a neutral merchant ship battling her way in a north-easterly direction. Unfortunately, it was not the ship we were looking for. We never did find the lost ship.

On another occasion we were returning to Campbeltown after a rough trip, which had taken us to about 20º west. Unfortunately, instead of a much looked forward to night ashore, we had to attend to our steering gear. The steering was situated in the stores and 'rope hold', which were aft of the engine-room. At sea a greaser visited the steering flat twice a day to attend to some grease cups, and once to oil points. At the same time a general check was carried out to see that nothing was working loose and so on. The 3rd engineer would also carry out a periodic inspection. The greaser had reported undue and unusual noises from the steering gear to the chief engineer.

The steering was the Hale-Shaw Martineau hydraulic gear, which contained two hydraulic rams which operated directly on the tiller head. Oil pressure could be created and maintained from zero to around 1600 lbs sq. inch when a by-pass or relief valve maintained the pre-set pressure. This same relief valve took care of overload when the rudder was subject to buffeting or severe shock from heavy seas. The Hale-Shaw pump was controlled by a steering telemotor which provided a hydraulic, frictionless means of transmitting the revolving motion of the steering wheel on the bridge to linear motion at the control valve of the Hale-Shaw pump. This pump was driven by an electric motor, which used the telemotor to vary the stroke.

Our problem turned out to be an almost seized shaft of about 3¼" diameter. It transpired that a brass bush in a casting containing a grease cup had not been drilled to allow the grease to get through to the bearing. We eventually got the shaft out, despite all the problems of a confined working space. Use was made of the lathe and bench drill in the workshop on the quay at Campbeltown. By 04.00 hours all was well and tested and we were off to sea again before daylight.

Many of our wanderings in the Atlantic were to put us in a position to be handy for convoys in the Atlantic, should they be attacked. We used to return to Campbeltown and go away up to Greenock for one reason or another. Fortunately the Navy seemed very fond of boiler cleaning. I say fortunately because it did mean some leave. Having to travel long distances on leave did have its problems. I remember one occasion when I was to call and see my parents in Colchester and collect my 4 ½ year old son David, to take him to his mother in Cornwall. We arrived at Liverpool Street station late evening in order to catch an overnight train from Paddington. One of London's major air raids was in progress, with the area round Liverpool Street station and St Paul's on the receiving end. Luggage made travel by tube very difficult and very few taxis were operating. Eventually I did get one, and after many diversions and reversing we got to Paddington. I certainly "took my hat off" to the taxi driver. Talking of hats, I sat in the taxi with my tin hat on and my son tucked under my arm with a suitcase, on end, on one side and my gas mask case in front of him for protection.

A couple of days later on the way back from Cornwall I arrived in London late evening at Paddington and took the tube to Kings Cross station. What an eye opener! Whole families were sleeping on the underground stations. Some were in three tier wooden bunks, others were stretched out on the platform, or sitting in circles eating their sandwich supper, or playing cards, talking, and no doubt praying.

My first Hogmanay in Scotland was a night of note. We had arrived in Greenock in *Restive* on 31st December 1940. *Restive* was due to dry-dock the following morning in Govan. I persuaded Lt. E. Richards to hop off home to Leith, by telling him that I would take care of the move up the Clyde at 06.00 hours the following morning. That evening two or three of us decided to take a train trip to Glasgow for an hour or so. I left the others in Glasgow to catch an early train back. Coming down the station steps was an old sea friend of merchant service days. He was on the way to spend Hogmanay with his sister. Unwisely I was persuaded to go along for just one "wee tot". Eventually I woke up with rug and pillow at the back of a settee – I looked at my watch and got the shock of my life – it was nearly five o'clock! I quickly got moving to find a number of people asleep. Upon heading for the bathroom I saw a light on in the kitchen, and closer investigation revealed the lady of the house making sandwiches. Another shock – it was five o'clock in the evening!!! I got on the telephone to an office at Greenock and was extremely relieved to discover that the move to the dry dock had been put off until the next morning. Back I went to Greenock with all haste, only to find the ship in darkness. The engineer aboard was not familiar with the procedure for transferring fuel oil. With a thick head second to none, much of the night had to be spent raising steam. However all went according to plan and within three or four days we were back at Campbeltown and within a few hours back at sea.

Around this time we picked up a small Lithuanian ship loaded with coal. Bad weather had put her out of commission. Sometime after taking her in tow back to Belfast, there came a stage when it was advisable to remove the crew. This was a well advised move, as she eventually turned over and sank.

3 – The Sinking Of The Rescue Tug *Englishman*

AROUND 14TH JANUARY 1941 we were out in company with the *Seaman*, a requisitioned tug belonging to United Towing of Hull, which was still sailing under the Red Ensign. She was under the command of Captain Owen Jones, ably assisted by the mate Jim Ryan. We lost contact when we were both searching for a damaged tanker off the Orkneys, on a dark and very stormy night. The following morning the *Seaman* was attacked by a German Focke-Wulf Condor, a large four engined long range aircraft, used mainly for reconnaissance work over the Atlantic. This aircraft made low passes and fired on the *Seaman* with machine guns. Jim Ryan, to use a time honoured expression, "stuck to his guns", in this case a machine gun on the bridge, and shot down the Condor on one of its low passes. The *Seaman* eventually picked up some survivors, including two or three Focke-Wulf employees, and landed them in Campbeltown. On 20th January 1941 we left Campbeltown in company with the *Englishman*. Once again we lost contact during the night. About mid-morning the next day our wireless people picked up a message from the *Englishman* saying she was being attacked by enemy aircraft. The message was not finished and nothing more was ever heard of the *Englishman* or her crew. This tragedy was a great blow to all at Campbeltown, especially as some of the crew had moved their families there from Hull. Captain Owen Jones and Chief Engineer Dodd had their families there too. I learned later that Owen Jones's son Ronald became a Humber pilot and Mr Dodd's son Ian became a fully qualified sea-going radio operator. *Restive* went on an immediate search for the *Englishman* without result. We wondered afterwards if the German aircraft had transmitted a message before crashing, giving details of the ship that had shot them down.

Campbeltown received attention from enemy aircraft too. On the first occasion mines on parachutes went wide of the entrance channel to the harbour and houses were damaged, people were injured and the Fiscal Mayor was killed. Later another enemy aircraft dropped bombs on the quayside, damaged the Royal Hotel, and some bombs hit other parts of the town. This was followed by a low level attack with machine guns.

At this time things were really getting hot for shipping in the Atlantic. U-boats were increasing in number and the surface raiders *Scharnhorst* and *Gueisenau* had been busy. By the time they entered Brest on 22 March 1941, they had sunk 22 allied ships totalling 115,000 tons. Some good news was the sinking of *U-47*, *U-99* and *U-100*. The captains were the three leading U-boat commanders of the day. German aircraft were taking an increasingly active part in attacking shipping around the British Isles and out into the Atlantic. This was made possible by the bases available after the Germans had overrun Norway, Denmark, Belgium and France. All this enemy activity kept rescue tugs very busy and took them to bases further and further from home.

From the very beginning of the war, U-boats gave the Atlantic a sinister sort of atmosphere. This was mainly due to their ability to remain submerged during the day, but still be able to observe without being seen. One day in *Restive*, we were almost in mid-Atlantic, heading north. The seas were fairly big, with a strong westerly wind and some rain. I was off watch and had taken a trip to the bridge for a 'change of scenery', a chat and some fresh air. We came to the top of one of those long Atlantic waves giving us a reasonable view around for a minute or so. We could not believe our eyes! About half a mile ahead and slightly to port was a surfaced U-boat going in the same direction. She too had just arrived at the top of a big wave. After a slight pause at the top, she slid away down the other side. We did not see her again. Perhaps she saw us and did not realise we were a rescue tug. It was generally reckoned that U-boats would not attack a rescue tug, as they liked to save their torpedoes for bigger ships. There were cases of ships under tow by rescue tugs being torpedoed again. When towing a disabled ship, we always had a sailor standing by the towing hook to knock out a quick release pin to let the rope go upon receiving a signal from the bridge. Otherwise the sinking ship could pull the rescue tug right over.

The main worries to shipping in war-time were U-boats, surprise by surface raiders, enemy aircraft, E-Boats in home waters, rogue mines and collisions between ships under blackout restrictions at night – particularly in convoys. Bad weather and fog, which cause enough trouble in peace time, are made worse by war conditions. Normally a ship in convoy carried a shaded blue light at the stern rail, which was just visible to the following ship. During this period merchant ship losses increased as more U-boats and long distance aircraft became available. For example, in January 1941 U-boats sank 39 ships and Condor aircraft sank 27 ships. The rescue tug service was kept very busy as a result of all these activities. I remember that we went through a stage of general despondency, partly due to the long periods of fruitless searches and the war news in general. Once away from the quayside, a ship becomes a complete self-contained world. News arrived in various ways such as the radio room, personal radios (although use was restricted at certain times), signals from passing ships, sometimes friendly aircraft and of course the 'galley wireless'. The 'galley wireless' is an expression that really arises from the fact that in most ships the galley is the centre of much gossip. Most people called there to collect food and drink, every hour of the day or night.

Normal practice was to have rescue tugs stationed at strategically important points, whether at an anchorage or at sea. To be in a handy position at sea meant being in the general vicinity of convoy routes, where they could quickly get to the position that the attack had taken place and hopefully recover any vessels that were still afloat after being damaged. Sometimes rescue tugs accompanied convoys. I can remember one or two occasions when *Restive* was instructed to join a homeward bound convoy when still well out in the Atlantic. In reasonably calm and clear weather it was surprising how far away the smoke from a convoy could be seen, which was long before the ships themselves were visible. Many ships were coal burners and had difficulties in controlling smoke emission, particularly when cleaning fires. Motor ships had problems too with their large diesel engines running at slow speeds. Before joining the rescue tug section I had been in five convoys, one from Freetown and four across the Atlantic. The first was homeward bound in a diesel engined tanker, *British Triumph*, and the others in a large old coal burner, *Sithonia*. This enabled me, on more than one occasion, to be able to explain to critics what the problems were, and although smoke was highly undesirable, it was pretty well unavoidable. Oil fired steam boilers were not quite the same problem. As long as oil temperatures and pressures were adjusted to meet a low-output requirement, using the correct sized nozzles, well cleaned, and a forced draught properly adjusted, all was well. On the other hand, it is quite easy to put up a smoke screen with suitable mal-adjustment of oil burning equipment. I remember seeing a film after the war called 'The Key' in which *HMRT Restive* was the 'star'. As much black smoke as possible seemed to be the order of the day, which was the very opposite of what should have happened.

Returning to Campbeltown was always popular as mail was awaiting us and we could post our letters. Mail from home is an extremely important item to a sailor, and more particularly so in wartime. Parents, wives and sweethearts looked forward to mail with the same urgent interest. At some stage we got word we were going to the Clyde for a refit and additional equipment.

4 – The Glasgow Blitz And Travelling By Train In War Time Britain

I WAS ABLE to get a letter off to my wife Kay with my 'kisses code', which meant, 'come to Glasgow'. She already knew the drill: get suitable digs and leave the address at St Enochs Hotel. We had already decided she should come to Campbeltown. At this time it wasn't too difficult to find digs in almost any built up area, as many people had gone to country areas to avoid air raids.

Restive called at Campbeltown on the 9 March 1941 and received instructions to proceed to Princes Dock, Govan, for a refit. We spent a few hours at Greenock, where I was able to telephone our office at St Enochs. They passed on the message from my wife that she had arrived from Cornwall and had found us some accommodation. It was an address in Kelvinside, Glasgow, which was quite close to Kelvin Museum. It was on the telephone, so I was able to contact her easily.

Restive went up to the dry dock on 13 March 1941. 'Chiefy' Richards went off to Leith, and I stayed behind to blow down the boiler and such like. Eventually I got ashore around 20.00 hours, and caught a train to the city centre and then one to Kelvinside. Whilst on the train, the air raid sirens declared their wailing warning. An elderly gent on the train advised me that Glasgow was more or less immune from an air raid because of the surrounding hills, clouds, anti-aircraft guns and so on. However, he was soon disillusioned. The Glasgow blitz of 13 and 14 March 1941 was soon under way. Things were getting a bit noisy and hectic by the time I found our accommodation. It was a large three-storey house, but we had to spend the two nights of the air-raid in the basement, under tables with mattresses on top. Getting back to *Restive* the following morning was quite an undertaking. I was later told that *Restive's* 3 inch anti-aircraft guns had had a busy night.

Four days leave enabled Kay and I and son Bruce to catch an overnight train to London. From there we travelled to Dedham to stay with my parents, where our older lad David was already staying. The train we were catching back to Glasgow was the 1900 hours from Colchester. My mother drove us to the station under the black-out conditions. After making sure there would be a train, she went off home.

We found ourselves on a rather lonely blacked-out station. The only signs of life were in the buffet refreshment bar, which had extremely dim lighting with one lady in attendance. Whilst getting a couple of drinks, I saw and purchased a packet of wafer biscuits and put them in my pocket. Just as we were getting onto the train I mentioned the biscuits to my wife. Unbeknown to me, things like this were hard come by, and so my wife decided very quickly to get more biscuits. She went to the carriage door, saw a porter nearby and asked him how long it would be before the train departed. "Four minutes mam" was the reply. She thereupon hopped off to get biscuits. I was attending to the luggage and making the baby comfortable, when I suddenly realized the train was moving off very quietly. No wife! I dashed to the corridor window to discover we had already left the station behind. In the blackout I found the emergency chain, and upon pulling hard it came halfway across the carriage before becoming effective and bringing the train to a stop. Our carriage was about half way along the train and when I looked out of the window I could see lights coming towards me from both ends of the train, which were being carried by the two guards. They met just in front of me, and I very quickly explained what had happened and why. One of them climbed up and got into the corridor and proceeded to tell me why I should not have stopped his train etc, etc. Name and address were requested. Whilst this was going on I looked out of the window, and approaching the rear of the train was a dim solitary light. However, the guard decided we must get on and we could not wait. Fortunately the train stopped at the next station – Marks Tey Junction. Here I got out, having arranged with the guard to take care of our luggage when they got to London. At Marks Tey it was arranged that I could return to Colchester by a parcel train which was waiting on the 'down' platform. They got word through to the Colchester station master's office, and I was able to speak to my wife and put her mind at rest and assured her I would soon be back.

Son Bruce and I were reunited with her in the station master's office. He had very kindly arranged to stop a Norwich to London express, which would get us to Liverpool Street station soon after the train we originally intended to travel in. I shall always remember the Norwich express slowing to a stop. The driver leaning out of his window and the fireman standing just behind him both silhouetted by the orange flare from the firebox. They looked anxious and were, I discovered later, relieved to know the unscheduled stop was only to pick up stranded passengers. It happened to be one of the nights when London's East End was having a full scale blitz. Our train finally came to a standstill just beyond Seven Kings station, where we remained for over two hours just behind the train we were on originally. When we finally got to Liverpool Street it was far too late to catch the night train from Euston to Glasgow. Staff at the Regional Transport Office at Liverpool Street made enquiries and discovered there was a train from Kings Cross station around 01.00 hours to Edinburgh. We eventually arrived in Edinburgh mid-morning and Glasgow around lunchtime.

Back to a very battered Glasgow, I fixed my wife and son up with a place to stay for the night, so that they could travel to Campbeltown the next day. I made my way back to *Restive* and received a ticking off from some shore based person because I was five hours late. I was not feeling in the best of form after a sleepless night and having had to leave my wife and son on their own in a blitz torn Glasgow. I'm surprised my unkind remarks did not land me in trouble as this character had far more gold braid than I. However, my captain and chief engineer thought I had done very well indeed in the circumstances and that is really all that mattered to me.

Restive set off very early the next morning for Greenock for de-gaussing off Sandbank, Dunoon, and compass swinging (adjusting) off Gourock in the 'tail of the bank'. However, before we got as far as Dumbarton various bearings on the main engine were running hot – the outcome of our refit. We had to go over the lot to readjust and get clearances right. Another sleepless night! Eventually we got to Campbeltown where I found my wife safely installed in a flat – once again thanks to the Lang family. The normal occupants of the flat had evacuated to relatives in the hills in case there was more bombing in Campbeltown.

The boson of *Restive*, unfortunately I have forgotten his name, was a real old time seafarer. I would say about 60 years of age with a lifetime at sea behind him. A stocky, strong man with a ruddy-cum-tanned complexion well lined with what one would call 'smile creases' and a twinkle in his eyes. I had great respect for him and loved to have a chat about things in general, but especially about the old days of "iron men in wooden ships". He was one of those men one felt the better for knowing. During one of our brief visits to Greenock in early 1941, we lay outside another two ships and remained there overnight. The next morning the boson was reported missing – of all the people not to be where he should be at a given time – no one could understand it. About mid-day someone coming aboard by the gangway spotted the boson floating between our ship and the next one. He was quickly taken from the water and laid on one of the cargo hatches of the coaster we were alongside. A doctor was summoned from a ship nearby, but there was nothing he or anyone else could do. The boson had obviously drowned during the night. He was in his underclothes – long sleeved vest and long pants. Many were the suggestions of what could have happened. He was not a 'drinker' so that was ruled out. As a highly conscientious man it was generally thought he was investigating an unusual noise – perhaps he was attempting to adjust ropes on his own – we shall never know.

5 – Enemy Activity At Sea Increases

ON 16 MAY 1941 Iceland severed its union with Denmark, and on 18 May the *Bismarck* and the *Prinz Eugen* sailed from Gdynia. These two events really spelt bad news. It was known that there was a lot of pro-German feeling in Iceland at that time and it was generally believed that Hitler was about to land forces there. Mr Churchill was quick to react and British Forces got there first in April 1941. This all had a direct bearing on rescue tug activities.

On 27 May 1941, after much activity by the British Navy and Fleet-Air Arm, *Bismark* and *H.M.S. Hood* were sunk during an engagement. We in *Restive*, along with other rescue tugs, were hopping about the Atlantic knowing that something 'big' was on, but not quite sure what. There were of course both naval forces and merchant shipping at high risk and the 'powers that be' wanted their little old rescue tugs handy in case somebody required a tow home. As a matter of interest, in 1943 the four rescue tugs, *Jaunty*, *Oriana*, *Nimble* and *Restive* towed the battleship *Warspite* to Gibraltar.

Restive and other rescue tugs returned to Greenock via Campbeltown. The same morning a destroyer came alongside the quay immediately ahead of *Restive* and landed survivors from the *Bismarck*. They were a sorry looking sight – no wonder when one reads of what they went through. After a night or so in Greenock, we went back to sea without calling at Campbeltown. Unbeknown to us, some U.S. transport ships with troops were crossing the Atlantic and a U-boat had sunk one of them on 21 May 1941. As the result of this, we were sent to Belfast with the U.S. transports.

I remember taking a stroll ashore in Belfast and eventually standing in front of the Grand Hotel. I was just making up my mind to ask a passer-by where the railway station was, in order to have a look at the broad gauge steam locomotives, when an American army lieutenant approached me. It was his first trip ashore this side of the Atlantic and he was interested to see something of Belfast. Conversation revealed he was a doctor from Texas, who had only recently been called up. After seeing the trains we found a comfortable pub and eventually arranged to meet the following evening, if we were still in Belfast.

During our pub session, we heard many rumours that the newly arrived American troops would be sent to the Republic of Ireland if the Germans made any attempt to land there. The following evening was a Sunday and pubs were closed. The American doctor had two officer colleagues with him, one of German extraction and the other Russian. While discussing what to do, two local senior citizens asked if we were perchance looking for somewhere to have a drink. Having explained details they invited us to their Working Men's Club. We found out later that they were World War One veterans who were working in the dockyard. Our thanks to them for a very entertaining night.

At the crack of dawn we were off again in *Restive*, into the North Atlantic and the usual searching. Long-range aircraft were being brought in to assist in these searches. In the beginning it was the Wellington Mark I and the Sunderland flying boat. If one of them had been detailed to assist say *Restive*, and the weather was suitable, they would make visual contact soon after daylight. After recognition signals and a short conversation by Aldus lamp, they would commence their search and could cover an area in an hour or so that would take us days. A number of ships and sometimes survivors were located in this way.

U-boat personnel were known later to refer to the first 18 months of the war as their "Happy Time". They did have another "Happy Time" for a while on the U.S. eastern seaboard, after America came into the War. Hunting became more difficult for U-boats after June 1941, as convoys were escorted right across the Atlantic. The Allies steadily built up anti-submarine escort forces, both on the sea and in the air, but it was not until the middle of 1943 that total overall training was considered adequate. Admiral Sir Percy Noble had been appointed Commander-in-Chief Western Approaches in 1941. He was able to organize bigger and better escort groups with enough men and ships to ensure that refits, leave periods and training could take place to maintain and increase the effective sea going escorts. Air protection received attention too. Anti-aircraft guns were mounted on most forms of ships. Some ships were fitted with catapults and carried a Hurricane fighter with a naval or R.A.F. pilot. After action, the fighter would hopefully land or 'ditch' alongside its own or a friendly ship and be rescued. As a matter of interest the German long distance FW200 Condor aircraft were flying from Bordeaux to Stavanger and vice-versa, to carry out reconnaissance weather reports and bombing of shipping in the Atlantic and Bay of Biscay.

You may well ask, "what has all this to do with rescue tugs?" It was among all these activities that the rescue tug had to operate, very often somewhat ignorant of what was really going on. We weren't given 'the big picture' at the time, but these major operations had a direct bearing on where rescue tugs were more or less permanently based.

In September 1940, the U.S. Navy passed over 50 First World War destroyers to the British. In return for this, they were allowed the use of certain bases, which included one in Newfoundland. These destroyers were easily identified by their four funnels. They did a grand job in the North Atlantic.

We eventually returned to Campbeltown and I was able to have another spot of leave. I joined wife Kay on the train to Greenock and then went down to Colchester by night-train. Three days later, we were back in Greenock. We parted on the train as she had to get back to our son Bruce in Campbeltown.

When I returned to *Restive* there was a new No 7, Sub-lieutenant Campbell of Glasgow. *Prudent*, the sister ship to *Restive*, was also in Greenock. Orders had been received that both rescue tugs were to join a convoy and proceed to a new base – St John's, Newfoundland. On our way we arrived at Campbeltown at around 05:30 hours, allowing the skipper and myself to go ashore for about half an hour. We popped around to my flat and I attempted to wake my wife. Banging on the front door, which was up steps at the back of the building, had no effect. I went around to the front, threw my gloves up one by one, but again to no effect. As a last resort I threw

5 – Enemy Activity At Sea Increases

up my hat, and that did the trick. We had only about five minutes for a quick conversation to discuss the bad news. I made a strong suggestion that she return to her mother's bungalow in Manaccan, a village in a remote part of Cornwall, mainly from a safety factor point of view. I had built an air-raid shelter into the hillside at the side of the bungalow whilst waiting to join the rescue tug section in August 1940. She agreed to return to Manaccan and also to give up the place we had in Falmouth. Little did I know that this would be the last time I would see her. It was a somewhat tearful parting, and I remember making the usual inane remark, "If anything happens to me, make sure the next bloke is well off." The wives in Campbeltown were still very aware of the loss of the *Englishman*.

Once back aboard *Restive*, we made our way with *Prudent* to join a west bound North Atlantic convoy. The weather was reasonably kind to start with, but we eventually ran into fog, where warm waters from the south meet the cold waters from the north.

We were in dead calm waters when the fog lifted, or we saw clear of it, and we could see *Prudent* and a few of the convoy ships. Soon we saw the coast of Newfoundland, not far from St John's. The massive rocky cliffs there must always have been a mariner's nightmare, particularly in the days of sailing ships. The entrance to the harbour is a comparatively narrow opening through the cliffs. I remember well the vast number of engine movements we had to perform to get us alongside the quay. In contrast, *Prudent* came in behind us and was tied up on about three engine movements. Our skipper was known as "Ting-a-ling McFunnel Casing", as he was very fond of the engine room telegraph, and at times it would move faster than we could work the engine to keep pace with him. A funnel casing is full of very hot air, so the name was appropriate for someone who always had a lot to say, some of which was hard to swallow. He was a 'big-ship' man – British India if I remember correctly, with a spell at some stage of his career as Harbour Master at Perim, between the Red Sea and the Gulf of Aden.

Our diesel-engined lifeboat was used as a duty boat for crossing the harbour on shore leave, and also for obtaining supplies from the store ship anchored at buoys in the middle of the harbour. The local people were very friendly and invitations to tea and for an evening game of cards were the type of hospitality we received. One gentleman with a cabin cruiser laid on the occasional trip out of the harbour and into a bay to the south. Here a first class barbecue was the order of the day.

Both *Prudent* and *Restive* went out on one or two search jobs. One evening, *Prudent* received a call to proceed to a Canadian Lakes boat that had run aground off the island of Miquelon. The C.O. of *Prudent* was Lt. Quinn R.N.R. The chief engineer was Lt. E Martin R.N.R. and the 2nd engineer was Lt. E. Pat Murray R.N.V.R. At the time of the call Pat Murray was ashore, so I took his place on *Prudent*. Rescue tugs on station could usually get underway in seven to ten minutes because the main engine was warmed through about every two hours – steering gear tested and so on. The bridge was kept well up to date with weather forecasts and all other information necessary for the C.O. to be fully in the picture regarding the area the rescue tug was likely to operate in.

The vessel off Miquelon turned out to be of about 2,500 tons and was carrying a cargo of coal. These lake steamers were of a distinctive construction, as the bridge was right up forward and the engine room right aft. The ship in question had run onto a sandy beach at high tide in fog. The crew was busy dumping coal over the side and about two high tides later we were able to pull them into deep water. Upon return to St John's I went back to *Restive*.

Sailing under the White Ensign allowed the commanding officer to make use of naval discipline. If the offence warranted it, he was able to take matters further than the more modest justice he could administer on the bridge. Just to get some idea on this subject, I can recall returning to the ship about 01.30 hrs and after passing a black-out curtain in an alleyway, I noticed that the electric lighting was down to a mere cigarette-like glow. Fortunately I was carrying a torch. A dash down to the stokehold showed that the fires were out, no one was on watch, and steam pressure was down to about 20 lbs. sq in. The engine-room also deserted and the dynamo was just ticking over. I made another quick dash to the stokehold, where I was able to get one fire working with the little steam left. Next I called the 3rd engineer, whose 'night aboard' it was. He went below to keep things going. Where were the greaser and fireman? A greaser and fireman shared a room and would normally be on watch together. Down at their quarters, I found that their door was locked. No response to knocking, so up to the bridge where the 'night aboard' deck officer was snoozing. We got a master key and returned to the lower decks. In their room we found the two men and two lady visitors, all 'out for the count' on rum! How they were able to smuggle two women aboard we never did find out. We had to turn out the next watch. The two 'rum' lads were charged before a commander ashore the following day and got, I believe, 92 days in a correction camp the Navy had ashore up country. We received two naval stokers to carry on with, until we could get T124T replacements.

6 – Iceland

NOT LONG AFTER this, *Restive* was instructed to proceed to Reykjavik, to tack onto the rear of an eastbound convoy. Eventually we left the convoy, returned to Iceland, and proceeded up the beautiful and vast Hvalfiordur. At the top of the fiord was the repair and submarine base ship *H.M.S. Hecla*. There was also an American repair ship similar to *Hecla* along with one or two tankers where fuel oil could be obtained. On 9th May 1941, the German submarine *U-570* surrendered and was taken to Hvalfiordur by the destroyer *H.M.S. Bulldog*. *U-570* was lying alongside *Hecla* when we arrived. We saw her leave later under her own power, with a Royal Navy crew who took her back to the U.K. She was a type VII c U-boat of 760 tons, later renamed *HMS Graph*.

Although Hvalfiordur was very impressive, there was nowhere to go ashore. An Icelandic drifter did daily runs to and from Reykjavik with naval personnel and mail. I once did the trip – and what a trip! It is about 50 miles to Reykjavik from Hvalfiordur, or "Hell Fiord" as it was often called. There was quite a gale blowing up the fiord, funnelled by the steep mountains either side. The drifter was meeting the waves head on, which made life for those of us crowded into the fish hold decidedly uncomfortable. This trip gave me a tremendous amount of admiration for people who fish for a living. I just do not know how they stick it.

One of our first trips to sea from Hvalfiordur took us within sight of Greenland. We were in fact searching an area south of that country for surviving ships, or personnel, from a convoy attacked by a number of U-boats. All we found was a fair amount of debris such as hatch covers, awning spars, splintered lengths of wood, etc. About this time the U-boat 'wolf pack' attack system was being developed. Briefly the U-boats were strung out in a long line roughly running north to south. The first U-boat to discover a convoy would shadow it and call up the remainder of the pack. They would remain submerged and arrange to attack as dusk approached, but make their major attack after dark on the surface.

There was however one weakness to this system, as the shadowing U – boat had to send out wireless signals to the rest of the pack. These signals were also picked up by Allied forces, enabling the Admiralty to plot the U-boat's position.

We eventually returned to Hvalfiordur to take on fuel and stores. Talking of stores we were informed upon arrival in Iceland that spirits were rationed to one bottle per officer per fortnight. There was something of a 'performance' to go through to draw our spirit ration, so it was decided to appoint an officer to take charge of the bond. This was normally a duty carried out by the C.O. and chief steward, but on this occasion it befell my lot to take charge of the bond in Iceland. The crew also requested, about this time, that we should have some form of shop aboard to supply tinned soup, biscuits, chocolate, sweets, razor blades and tinned fruit. Firstly I turned one of the drying rooms on the port side into a lockup shop. Everyone was then asked to contribute £1, with which I purchased the initial stock from *Hecla*. The selling price was arranged to show a small profit, so it wasn't long before the shop showed a profit, and we were able to pay back the original investment paid by the 'shareholders'. The chief petty officer I dealt with on board *Hecla* was extremely helpful and we became quite good friends. In peacetime he ran one or two grocer's shops in Glasgow.

When we first went into Reykjavik we lay alongside a minesweeper, whose crew were able to advise us of the situation ashore. At that time Iceland was 'dry' and alcoholic drinks were unobtainable. Duty free tots could be obtained at a mixed officers' club in the suburbs of Reykjavik. In the city was the Borg Hotel for officers, where dancing was permitted, but not alcohol. The drill was to take your own booze in a small bottle and pop it into the non-alcoholic beer available. Also at this time there was a non-fraternisation policy in Iceland, because of the 'Occupation' by Allied forces. The Germans had done quite a lot in Reykjavik pre-war, such as piping hot water around the town from natural hot springs. They also built the library and university.

On our first trip ashore we had the usual look around the

town and finished up at the Borg Hotel. As soon as we entered the dance area it was obvious that the sexes were segregated. On the right, in the corner, was the dance band run by a rather, as we thought, mysterious Englishman. On the same side were all the "belles" of Reykjavik. We soon got ourselves settled and into conversation with other officers. Then, without warning, a female hand was laid upon my shoulder. I was even more surprised when I was addressed by my Christian name! This girl and her sister had worked in Copenhagen before the war at the Animal Kruger Club. I was there on the *S.S. Darcoila* in March 1939, when we were discharging cargo from the Far East. The 2nd mate and I used to go to this club often and this girl remembered me from there. My newly rediscovered friend invited me to meet her mother and "again my sister." In order not to break the non–fraternisation ban and possibly get her hair shaved off, she gave me her address and went off. I was instructed to follow by taxi ten minutes later. Everything went according to plan, and I suddenly found I had friends in Reykjavik.

This contact proved very useful for flogging our booze. The people getting caught were those going ashore with the odd bottle in their pocket, and who were stopped and searched soon after leaving the quay or jetty. To draw our ration upon arrival in Reykjavik at anytime, I had to make out a form to be signed and stamped by our C.O. and myself. Then away to the base ship *H.M.S. Boldur*, where said form had to be signed and stamped by the executive officer, before proceeding along to the man in charge of the N.A.A.F.I. who actually issued the spirits. My Icelandic friends had introduced me to a local gentleman who owned two taxis, and as a sideline dealt in hooch – an Icelandic bootlegger no less! I remember being in his house one day when he gave me a drop of local brew from somewhere inland. Real firewater if ever there was. Enough to say I used to share the proceeds out with fellow members of the wardroom, having deducted 10% for my trouble!

On the odd occasion we used to launch our motor lifeboat and go fishing in Reykjavik outer harbour. We would first of all get someone to go to the beach, on the east side of the harbour, and collect mussels from the rocks. Upon return to the *Restive* the bucket of mussels would be taken to the engine room and boiled by a steam jet. This made them easier to open when fishing. After lunch Chiefy Richards and I, with usually a sailor and fireman to steer and work the engine, would proceed to our fishing ground. We would then let down our lines, which were attached to a stout wire carrying three lines with hooks and baits. Iceland was noted for its fishing grounds and the outer harbour at Reykjavik is no exception, with the result that we could pull out three fish every time at about five minute intervals. Another set of baited hooks would be ready, so our productivity was increased. We could catch a meal for all hands, which led to a saving in the various mess funds, so that any surplus could be shared out where appropriate. Another form of fishing worthy of mention was carried out on the high seas. We very often went out with an escort which carried depth charges. One depth charge over the stern would produce enough fish, of all shapes and sizes, for both ships, for days.

When Germany attacked Russia on 22 June 1941, Iceland suddenly became even more important as a base. Churchill and Roosevelt decided to send as much aid as possible to Russia, and gave way to Stalin's demand that this aid should be shipped via the Arctic Ocean to Murmansk or Archangel. When the Russian convoys started from Iceland they were identified by the letters PQ outward bound and QP on return. The first PQ convoy from Reykjavik to Archangel sailed on 28th September 1941.

We were kept very busy working from Reykjavik. One job was to search for a Norwegian whale factory ship, which we eventually found with the aid of an escort. Assistance was not required, as they were able to get steam up on the starboard engine – even though they had been torpedoed in the port engine-room. They were carrying a cargo of oil and a deck cargo of war material. We stayed with them to Reykjavik in case of further trouble.

Not so long after that we were south of Iceland searching for a torpedoed tanker when we ran into some extremely bad weather. At

03:45 I was in the galley getting tea and sandwiches before going on watch at 8 bells. Suddenly there was a bang from the engine-room accompanied by high pressure steam escaping. I ran along to the after deck entrance to the engine-room. I say ran because that was what I was trying to do, but moving around was not easy in bad weather. The ship was rolling and the heavy seas were breaking over the side and across the engine-room skylights, which were all battened down and blacked out of course. The rear door to the engine-room faced aft. Once opened there were metal steps leading down to the top platform, which ran around the bottom of the cylinder casings. A blackout canvas curtain hung just inside the door. When I opened the door I was met with a hot blast of steam, which made it impossible to enter the engine-room. By this time I was aware that the escaping steam was escaping intermittently at intervals corresponding to engine revolutions, and the noise left no doubt that it was high-pressure steam. This meant that it could only be something wrong at the high-pressure piston end of the engine. Why hadn't the 3rd engineer or the greaser stopped the engine? Had they been burnt? I made my way as quickly as possible to the boat deck, where an external valve had an extension to the main stop on the boiler top. Here I was able to shut off the steam to the main engine. The noise and the main engine stopped, so I went as quickly as possible to the stokehold to make sure that the fires had been turned off and things were under control at that end. Then to the engine room via the stokehold expecting to find somebody injured. Instead I found a very seasick and frightened 3rd engineer. He was a newcomer to the ship and had not yet got his tug sea legs. The greaser had been away calling the next watch. By this time just about everybody was running around wanting to know what was wrong. A ship without power in that weather was no joke. Apart from the discomfort, the ship could have floundered.

It took a little while to find the trouble. We eventually found that the high pressure cylinder cover had split about three quarters of the way around, just inside the ring of holding down bolts, and had lifted slightly rather like an oyster. We then saw the cause.

There is a relief valve, spring loaded, at the top and bottom of all steam pistons. If for any reason water got into the piston, carried over from the boilers by what is commonly known as priming, it cannot be compressed and could cause serious trouble without an escape route. In this case the boiler had primed owing to the ship rolling and pitching. Water got through to the piston and instead of opening the relief valve, as the piston came to the top of its stroke, the pressure created lifted the valve seat, which was originally sunk into the cylinder cover casting. So the valve itself was unable to open and away went the cylinder cover. We were planning to work the engine as a compound, using the medium and low-pressure cylinders, when a signal was received that another rescue tug was around and would tow us to Stornoway. I believe the rescue tug that turned up was the *Tenacity*. Unfortunately, there was no suitable spare cylinder cover for us there. After consultation with the base engineer, our best option seemed to be to have one made locally. We were taken to a rather large general smithies shop. The gentleman in charge advised us he could make one, whereupon the damaged part was transported to his workshop. We called back after a couple of days and there was a very fine makeshift cover almost finished. He had cut it out from a steel plate about 1½ inches thick, heated it on his forge, beaten a hollow in the middle, drilled the dozen or so 2 inch holding down stud holes, drilled and tapped the holes for the safety valve and skimmed the whole lot up on a large and ancient lathe – a truly remarkable job under the circumstances.

Whilst this was going on we did see something of Stornoway, which was an interesting mixture of fishing port and country market town. We noticed on market day that Gaelic was spoken by the farmers or crofters. Their sheep provide the wool for the world famous Harris Tweed. Some R.A.F. officers billeted at the local hotel were kind enough to entertain us. One evening we were taken across to the Kyle of Lochalsh by the local ferryboat, to a dance. We spent an uncomfortable night sleeping on the ferry, until its return trip in the morning.

Far too quickly we were off again back to Reykjavik. About this time we had to proceed to a point somewhere not too far from Jan Mayen Island to look for a Russian ship. Fortunately the weather was reasonably kind and the ship, a tramp steamer, was located without too much trouble. For reasons I have now forgotten, it was decided I would go to the ship in our motorboat and attempt to find out what was wrong. When I arrived at the Russian ship, I found the Jacobs ladder they had put over the starboard side, just about mid-ships. There was a fairly heavy sea running, lifting the motor-boat fifteen to twenty feet at the crest of a wave. The ideal situation was to jump onto the ladder when the motorboat was on the crest of a wave. This I managed, and proceeded up the swinging ladder to the deck. The only person present was a young lad. He stood back when I climbed over the rail, as if 'Old Nick' himself had arrived! He pointed towards the bridge and led the way up to the mate's room, on the boat deck. The mate could, I suppose, be called a typical Russian. He had cropped hair, a heavy jowled red face, was overweight and probably in his mid fifties. He was spread out in an armchair at his desk quite close to the door, which was on his left. I was not invited into the room but left out in the extremely cold wind. The sea spray on my duffle coat had long ago frozen solid. From his limited English and with the help of a Russian-English dictionary, the story unfolded itself. They had come as far north as possible to avoid U-boats and German aircraft, and had been mixed up with both bad weather and ice flows. As a result of this, the ship had more or less broken its back just forward of the boiler room. In fact I had noticed some buckling of the deck when I first stepped onto it. All the Russian wanted was a tow to Akureyri in the north of Iceland. I went back to the Jacobs ladder, which was a signal to our boat to return and pick me up. What a job it is in heavy seas getting back aboard one's own lifeboat! Back on board *Restive*, I informed the C.O. that the only thing requested was a tow, and that technical assistance or portable salvage pump were not required. Eventually we got connected up with 120 fathoms of 18 inch rope, and about the same length of doubled 2 inch wire hawser.

Akureyri is about 45 miles from the sea at the head of Eyja Fjord, and had a population of around 1500. It was a popular holiday resort with Reykjavik people and one of the few places in Iceland that has trees. Fishing was the main industry. We spent one night alongside and found there was very little entertainment ashore. However it did present an opportunity for a good long walk. We met some army people ashore who invited us for a drink, and we returned the compliment by inviting them back to *Restive* where a good time was had by all. I vaguely remember that we had borrowed a two-wheeled handcart, normally used for carrying fish, to transport two of the army gentlemen back to their billet. Upon return to the quayside this barrow found its way on to our after deck. Because of this, we had an early morning visit from the local Bobbie and two army Red Caps. However all was explained over a tot or two and everyone went happily about their business.

During this time the Russians, with some local assistance from a small shipyard, had made their ship more sea worthy so that they could use their own main engine, but for some reason, not their steering gear. We were advised when the Russians were ready to leave for Reykjavik. Unfortunately, when we were warming through our main engine, the casting containing the Edwards air pump, two feed pumps and two bilge pumps broke away from the main engine. All five of these pumps were driven from the high-pressure crosshead of the main engine. *Restive* was towed by the tanker *British Ensign* to Reykjavik, with *Restive* acting as rudder to the bigger ship. When our C.O. went aboard to make arrangements, he discovered that his old school friend Captain Hutchinson was master of the tanker. It was a rather stormy trip right around the Icelandic Cape Horn. As it was towards the end of the summer, it was getting dark around mid evening. In these waters in summertime the nights are quite light whereas in winter the hours of daylight are extremely short. We had a corvette as escort and upon nearing Reykjavik our ship was taken in tow to the dockyard.

During the couple of days our repairs were being carried out, our

Icelandic friends took the chief engineer and I a few miles inland for picnics, and to see the natural hot water springs, hot pools and geysers. This natural hot water is used not only for central heating in Reykjavik but also to heat large areas of greenhouses nearby. We did see the two active volcanoes, *Hecla* and *Katta*, in the distance. Iceland is mainly a mountainous country with many permanent snow-caps and glaciers where nothing grows. Fortunately the Gulf Stream brings milder weather to certain coastal areas, otherwise the whole country would be covered in ice.

In the spring of 1941 Churchill and Roosevelt signed the Lend-Lease Agreement which provided Britain with a huge amount of much needed war equipment. Rescue tugs were included. Shortly afterwards in the summer of 1941, the American destroyers *Green, Reuben, James* and *Kearney* attacked U-boats in the North Atlantic. In late October 1941 *Restive* was directed to search for, and render assistance to, the *Kearney* which had been torpedoed off the south of Greenland. We eventually found her in pretty rough weather and poor visibility. The crew was still aboard and we had to launch our motorboat to put a rope aboard. Thankfully we were well protected by our escort until we reached Liverpool, where a harbour tug took over. We took fuel and water during the night, and eventually left for Campbeltown.

We arrived late evening and got tied up alongside the jetty around 21.00 hours. After a wash and brush up and change of clothes, it was off to Chiefy's room for a drink and chat. The silence was heavenly after weeks of being chucked around by the violent rolling and pitching of the ship and the noise of tons of water roaring over the forecastle. The ship would shudder when it had mounted a big wave and dropped into the wave trough following. It would then be smacked by the next big wave and up would go the bows again. The after-end of a rescue tug was very low in the water, and was subject to a good old battering in bad weather, if the sea was coming from either starboard or port quarters. Waves would break right across the engine-room skylight. A following sea could be unhealthy too. All accommodation entrances at main deck level had high steps below the doors, because it was not unusual in bad weather to see water rushing up the alleyways when the bows were down and the stern up. When the propeller was lifted partly and sometimes nearly fully from the water, the main engine would race away before the throttle could be closed. This would cause noise and vibration throughout the ship. However, these triple expansion steam engines ran at about 112 revolutions per minute at normal cruising speed of 13 knots and were extremely quiet in normal conditions.

7 – A Personal Tragedy

THE PEACEFUL CHAT and drink were interrupted by the arrival of mail in the wardroom. When my mail was handed to me I noticed the familiar writing of my wife and my parents. There were also letters from friends, some newspapers and a telegram. I went to my room to quietly read all the mail – people always seem to isolate themselves when they have mail to read. First one puts all letters in order by stamp date and so one gets the 'news' in chronological order. For some unknown reason I read my wife's letters first and then opened the telegram. I think I read it at least three times before I could really comprehend what it said. It simply stated that on 28th October 1941 at 8.37pm, my wife and her mother had been killed in an air raid. Son Bruce was seriously injured, with little hope. Why a single bomb should have been dropped on an isolated bungalow remains a mystery. The telegram was sent by my sister-in-law Mrs Meg Roberts. She ran the Shipwrights Arms public house, which is on the Helford River in Cornwall. I won't dwell on the subject – it just makes me feel numb and sick. About one o'clock in the morning I walked up to the Campbeltown police station to try and find out if Bruce was still alive. They were extremely kind and helpful. First they rang the police station in Helston and got some more detailed information. They then rang the cottage hospital in Helston and after a few words handed me the telephone. It was the night sister who, as kindly and sympathetically as possible, informed me that Bruce had not regained consciousness and had died four days after his mother and grandmother.

The following day I was granted a week's compassionate leave. It took a day by bus, boat and train to get to Glasgow, where I spent the night with old friends the Kenny family. The following day I travelled to Colchester, where I was able to spend a few hours with my parents and older son David. Then off to Cornwall. I arrived late in Falmouth, and had the wartime difficulty of finding a place to stay for the night. The next morning I decided to visit

Falmouth Parish Church where we were married. Kneeling in there and praying really brought things to a head, and I had a good old cry. After that, I took the bus to Helford River and the one-man ferryboat across to the Shipwrights Arms, where I was to stay. After lunch, the Roberts and I walked to St Antony's Church to see the grave, and then to where the bombing took place. The hole in the garden was larger than the area of the bungalow. The bomb was of the type intended for shipping, with the fuse delayed so that it would go off after passing though a few decks. This meant that it passed through the roof of the house and detonated after it reached the foundations. How final everything was.

8 – The Coastguard Cutter *Alexander Hamilton*

UPON RETURNING TO Campbeltown, I found that some repairs and a boiler clean had been carried out on *Restive*. We had a new C.O. Lt. J.W. Evenden R.N.R., and a new No. 2, Sub Lt. Campbell R.N.V.R. On our return to Iceland, we found that winter was really setting in, and there was only daylight from mid-morning until mid-afternoon. The seas around there were awful, with bad weather being swept by a never-ending succession of gales. In winter these gales take the form of snow-laden blizzards cutting visibility to nil. The northwest of Iceland is just inside the Arctic Circle, so additional hazards are ice flows, icebergs, and the problem of snow and spray forming ice on the ship's rigging and super-structure. On trips going south-westerly from Reykjavik, we often encountered fog. This was caused by the Gulf Stream coming up from the south meeting the cold water from Polar Regions. Fog, icebergs, pack ice and even other shipping can give a ship's captain some sleepless nights. To make matters even worse, compass needles could not be trusted on the approach to Reykjavik harbour, or south of the entrance to Hvalfjordur. The high iron content of nearby mountains caused magnetic distortion. Twice in our early days there, *Restive* received some bumps on the bottom when returning to Reykjavik under conditions of bad visibility. We were told that some aircraft and a few ships were lost through this magnetic phenomenon. The local airport was at Keflavik, south of Reykjavik. At the time we arrived in Iceland, there were two or three RAF fighter squadrons stationed there. They were 'resting', after the hectic time they had had in France and the Battle of Britain. However, we did gradually learn that they weren't getting much of a rest, as they had a very tough job on their hands seeking the enemy aircraft that were attacking the North Atlantic convoys. The 'galley wireless' also suggested they would be handy, along with the navy and the army, if the Germans attempted to force the Allies to leave Iceland.

In January 1942, *Restive* was instructed to locate and recover an American coastguard cutter named the *Alexander Hamilton*. She had been torpedoed whilst on convoy duty and was still afloat to the south of Greenland. These coastguard cutters were similar in size and appearance to a corvette. We eventually located her and discovered her crew had been taken off. The weather was, as usual, very bad. This made launching our motor lifeboat something of a job. Getting on board a ship with no crew on also had its problems. When this situation arose, the motorboat would be swung out, and the engine started just before it entered the water. Whilst this was going on, the rescue tug would be steaming in a port turn so that the motorboat could be dropped into the calm stretch of water created on the port side of the rescue tug. Usually the No.1 would be at the tiller, and one of the engineers would control the throttle, and the ahead and reverse levers. Weather conditions would determine what action we needed to take when we reached the casualty. If the No.1 and the engineer were going to be in the boarding party, a trained coxswain would be concerned with getting the towing gear aboard the casualty, making fast, and take steps to ensure the towing wires could not 'shape' or wear through. The engineer officer would concern himself with seeing what could be done to check water entering compartments or holds, other than the one damaged. For example, I can recall cases where the casualty had been torpedoed aft of midships or engine room, but the engine and boiler rooms had flooded from water entering by the propeller shaft tunnel. Fortunately all ships have a remote control at the top of the engine room by which the tunnel door can be closed. A portable pump could then be manhandled aboard so that the engine room spaces could be pumped dry. The casualty then has a far better chance of survival with the additional buoyancy obtained.

   In the case of the coastguard cutter, those who went aboard were able to do little more than close accommodation doors at deck level where the sea was inclined to enter, as the ship had a ten to fifteen degree list to port. These doors had strong clips and were more or less watertight once closed. The torpedo had hit the port side and blown a hole in the engine-room. These U.S. coast guard cutters were very strongly built to enable them to work in waters around

Alaska, where they could have ice problems. They had unusually large wardrooms to accommodate courts so that trials concerned with customs and fishing matters could be held in such isolated places.

Once the towing gear had been made fast the motorboat returned to *Restive*. Lt. Evenden then went slowly ahead and played out the 100 or so fathoms of double towing wire, and then the 120 fathoms of 18 inch manila towrope. Next came the critical moment of taking the strain on the towropes to commence the actual towing. This was not at all easy in bad weather. A 'snatch' on the towing gear could break the towing wires, and this would mean the whole business of hauling in the towing ropes, returning to the casualty and the difficult procedure of connecting up again. I remember one C.O. who often broke ropes, on long tows and also on short tows for entering port. We were joined by the rescue tug *Frisky* under the command of Lt. Harry Tarbottom R.N.R. After the usual 'rough and tumble' of towing in bad weather at slow speed, we got within sight of the entrance to Reykjavik and preparations were being made to shorten the towropes. That is, to take in the manila 18 inch rope, have one end of the towing wire round the capstan aft, and the other end made fast to one of our bollards. This gave control over the length of the tow wire, as it could then be progressively shortened as required until a harbour tug, or tugs, took over.

The coastguard cutter had taken on more 'up list' during the final night of towing. No one was sure what happened, but as the crew were starting to shorten the tow, she turned turtle and remained afloat, but with the keel uppermost. Eventually the Americans decided to sink her, as she was then just another hazard to shipping. From our point of view it was a great shame, because without any doubt whatsoever our great pride and joy was to arrive with our casualty and hand over to the salvage section.

We proceeded to Hvalfjordur for fuel, stores and to stock up the canteen. I had the pleasure of a chat and a drink with the chief petty officer who supplied these goodies. Heinz soup '47 Varieties' was the popular item and always in great demand. Another interest to me were the ex U.S. fan funnelled destroyers. Many of them had Canadian crews and the wardrooms seemed to be well stocked with Canadian rye whisky. Usually the doctor was in charge of the officers' bond. I made it my business to get to know one or two of them and, as a result, could usually purchase a couple of cases of rye.

There were often times when we were at anchor and on immediate notice. This situation cancelled shore leave. To pass the time, playing card games, darts, chess and reading were popular activities. The ship's library was changed fairly frequently by the amenities organisations afloat in ships like *HMS Hecla*, in out of the way bases, and in large permanent naval bases. Woollen goods such as roll neck jerseys, balaclava head coverings, large woollen stockings and gloves, were given out. These were donated by voluntary organisations and individual ladies. I had a large white jersey on one of these occasions and found a "good luck" message pinned inside, with the address of the donor who lived in Hamilton, Scotland. I wrote a note of thanks and assurance that the jersey was being put to good use. The lady kept in touch throughout the war, and I called on her when on demob leave, to offer my humble thanks. The knitted items and food parcels were very highly appreciated by all the services – particularly in out of the way places where few home comforts were available. It was especially kind as the folks in the U.K. were on rations and short of things themselves.

Occasionally we supplied fuel oil at sea to the ex-US destroyers who had run low but were still under their own steam. They were on convoy escort duty from Halifax, Nova Scotia and would normally hand over to other escorts when they reached the south of Iceland and then make for Hvalfjordur. They did carry enough fuel for the trip but ran short if there was a lot of enemy activity. If a major attack by U – boats developed, escort vessels would have many more miles of extra steaming to deal with the enemy, and very often at full speed. Fuel consumption rises at an alarming rate once a ship is pressed over its designed economical speed. When taking fuel under these circumstances the supplying ship would get a towing wire connected to the ship requiring fuel, and at the same time take a fire hose end. As the supplying ship (in our case *Restive*) steamed slowly ahead both the towing wire and the fire hose would be paid out until a safe distance had been reached. The supplying ship would then 'take the weight', and continue to steam slowly ahead to keep the wire rope reasonably taut. This allowed both ships to maintain a fixed distance apart and not put any strain on the lengths of hose – usually standard fire hose. This heavy fuel oil had to be heated for handling, so all the bunker tanks had steam coils to heat the oil to flow temperature, as and when required. Hot oil would then be pumped to the other ship, which would have made suitable arrangements to receive it. This same oil transfer pump on a rescue tug was occasionally used to pump oil on the sea, to help calm very rough seas when assisting a distressed ship.

The assurance class rescue tugs had a fuel transfer pump in the stoke-hold, normally used for transferring fuel oil from seven bunker tanks to a central tank in front of the stoke-hold, known as the 'daily service tank'. The oil was taken from this tank by one of two fuel oil pumps and passed under pressure to the boiler burners suitably filtered and heated. Combustion of this atomised oil was assisted by heated forced draught air.

9 – *HMS Sheffield* Hits A Mine

ABOUT THIS TIME, *Restive* was instructed to proceed to the assistance of the cruiser *H.M.S. Sheffield* at Seydhisfjördhur on the east coast of Iceland. When we arrived we found *Sheffield* at anchor near a small fishing port of 900 people. It was surrounded by formidable bare rock mountains, snow covered in winter and snow capped in summer. It was a reasonably safe anchorage weather-wise, but there was the risk of discovery by enemy reconnaissance aircraft. A further risk was the few nationalistic Icelanders who considered their country had been 'occupied' by the Allied Forces. However, the Icelanders I got to know seemed delighted with all the extra business the 'occupation' had brought them.

One of the many hazards to shipping, around the southeast and east of Iceland in particular, was the rogue anti-ship mine. Mines contained a safety device to deactivate them when they were drifting at random. When anchored in minefields, they were buoyant just below the surface, creating a pull on the anchor wire, which compressed a spring that activated the mine. In daylight, a drifting mine could usually be sighted and avoided. If circumstances permitted, steps were taken to blow it up. However, in darkness they were difficult to spot and could be struck head on. If they travelled along the side of the ship, the broken anchor wire could get caught in the propeller, making the wire taut again and re-activating the mine. The next time it bumped into the ship, the mine would explode. This is apparently what happened to *H.M.S. Sheffield*.

Making her way at high speed from Scapa Flow to help protect a Russian bound convoy, *H.M.S. Sheffield* was making a starboard turn when her outer port propeller caught the wire of a rogue mine. The explosion blew a hole in the port quarter about 37 feet by 21 feet. The flag officer's quarters were destroyed and his Royal Marine batman was killed. On the bridge at the time was the flag officer, Vice Admiral Bonham-Carter. When *Restive* arrived alongside, Lt. Evenden reported aboard *Sheffield* where he discussed the plans to get her to Scapa Flow and the Tyne. To temporarily patch the hole in *Sheffield*, bulks of timber were required from the store in Reykjavik. *Restive* proceeded at once back to Reykjavik to collect about a dozen bulks of timber, of about 45 feet long by 2 feet square. Certain other equipment was taken aboard, as well as two naval divers from the salvage section. Back at Seydhisfjördhur, *Sheffield's* own personnel had carried out much preparatory work. Large eyebolts were fitted to the timber on *Restive's* deck, whilst similar fastenings were fitted by *Sheffield's* personnel to the canvas, to make the whole lot fast with wire hawsers through the eyebolt. *Sheffield* had been trimmed well down by the bow so that as much of the damage at the stem as possible was out of the water. When *Sheffield* was finally considered sea-worthy, she sailed for Scapa Flow accompanied by a destroyer escort and *Restive*. About this time Lt. J. W. Evenden was having tooth trouble. The medical people on *Sheffield* very kindly took him in hand, and had to remove most of his top teeth. We were invited for gin once or twice in *Sheffield's* wardroom.

10 – A Stormy Night In Hvalfjordur – Rescuing the *El Illeo*

AFTER TAKING FUEL oil, *Restive* left for Reykjavik. Unfortunately we soon had to put into Scrabster Bay because of a leaking boiler tube. Examination revealed that a tube in the top row on the port furnace was leaking badly, and a new tube stopper had to be fitted. The boiler was shut down and then blown down by seacock until the water level was below the offending tube. A safety valve was then opened to get rid of the remaining steam as quickly as possible. The furnace front was removed, so that boards and wet sacks could be used along the furnace bottom and in the combustion chamber. To do the repair, I went along to the combustion chamber with a set of steel tubes and copper discs and a nut to fit the 1¼ inch rod. Getting to the back of the furnace, standing on a box, reaching up to get the washers and nut on, all had to be done as quickly as possible because of the heat. When the job was completed I made a hurried exit, ensuring that all my tools were removed. The boiler was then topped up with fresh water and steam raised, the safety valve reset, and the ship was able to get underway. We proceeded to Hvalfjordur for more fuel oil, stores and so on. When winter comes along, the weather in Iceland can change literally at the 'drop of a hat'. For example, I remember one time when a few of us were preparing to go ashore at around 17.30 hours. Within about 20 minutes a force 10 gale had us steaming half ahead with two anchors down.

A night never to be forgotten was 15 March 1942. Anchored in Reykjavik's outer harbour, we were on immediate notice, and so no shore leave was allowed. The weather was wet with strong winds, slowly increasing to force 12 plus. This meant that we had to steam with both anchors down to hold our position. Also in the outer harbour were merchant ships at anchor, waiting to form a convoy to Russia. By about 20.00 hours the gale had reached hurricane force, estimated to have reached 135 miles per hour. Merchant ships started dragging their anchors. Very soon one drifting ship would catch the anchor chain of another, and it was not long before

17 merchant ships were ashore. Some were founding and beginning to break up. *Restive* was instructed to go to the assistance of, I suppose, basically any ship she could assist. Fortunately we had Lt. J. W. Evenden as our C.O. He had been with the United Towing Co. of Hull pre-war and knew an awful lot about ocean tugs and bad weather. Looking back, it is amazing that *Restive* survived the night.

One ship that was really in a bad way was the Panamanian vessel *El Illeo*. It was obvious that the ship could not be saved and so it was decided to get the master and crew off, if at all possible. The 135 m.p.h. wind was hurling tremendous seas over a now badly listing *El Illeo*. Only a man with the skill of Lt. Evenden could get an ocean tug the size of *Restive* anywhere near the doomed vessel. There was the risk of serious damage from going aground ourselves, collision with the *El Illeo*, and danger from other vessels adrift, some of whom were fighting for survival under their own power.

On an occasion like this the tension and strain on the bridge is transmitted throughout the ship, and everyone had to play his part to the utmost, particularly when there were one or more lives at stake. This occasion was no exception. In the engine room and boiler room, bad weather brings on problems mainly associated with retaining one's balance, and controlling the main engine when it starts to race when the propeller has lifted out of the water. Routine work must go on to keep engine and boilers functioning correctly. Bearing or boiler trouble is best avoided during a hurricane! Engine requirements are transmitted from the bridge by a visual telegraph, and also a bell to draw attention. The bridge and engine room telegraph are identically marked, with STOP, STANDBY, SLOW AHEAD, HALF AHEAD and FULL AHEAD written on the right hand side. FINISHED WITH ENGINES, SLOW ASTERN, HALF ASTERN and FULL ASTERN were written on the left. When the ship was being manoeuvred, the bridge required the movement to be both accurate and quick. Signals received in the engine room are confirmed by a stand-by greaser or fireman.

All telegraph messages were entered into the movements' book, with the time received, such as: Standby 03.28, Slow Ahead 03.45, Half Ahead 03.49, Stop 04.03, Slow Astern 04.06, Full Astern 04.10, Full Ahead 04.12, and Stop 04.14. Shorthand symbols were used instead of words.

In the case of the *El Illeo,* our C.O. would position *Restive* so that she was head on to the sea, and gently drop astern to get into a position where the crew of the ship in distress could jump aboard in small numbers. *Restive* would repeatedly steam 'Full Ahead', and then drop back again until the stern was in position for some more of the *El Illeo* crew to jump. In this way, even under atrocious weather conditions, the whole crew was rescued. Lt. Evenden was awarded the M.B.E. in official recognition of this operation. To complete the story of the *El Illeo,* she was eventually recovered and patched up by the Royal Navy salvage section, based in Iceland. Later, she was towed to the Orkneys by the new *H.M.R.T Saucy,* commanded by Lt. Evenden. What he had to say about that tow is interesting:

> "She (*El Illeo*) was 2000 tons overloaded and floating on her 'tween decks. They (RN salvage section) having welded all the hatches in the 'tween decks, so virtually the 'tween decks was the bottom of the vessel. I was given instruction from the navy that on no account was she (*El Illeo*) to roll on passage. So I turned her round through two depressions heading to sea between Iceland and the Orkneys and got her there. During passage I was leaking fuel oil through our lavatories to break the seas for her".

As soon as the crew of *El Illeo* were landed at Reykjavik, we were instructed to go to the assistance of *S.S. Vestland*. Once again *Restive* headed for the outer harbour and the confusion of hurricane conditions. When we found the *S.S. Vestland,* she was dragging her two anchors and almost ashore. Again amazing seamanship by Lt. Evenden made it possible to get a towrope aboard the distressed vessel, keeping clear of her anchor chains, and eventually getting her in tow whilst she picked up her anchors, then assisting her to a safe anchorage.

Sub. Lt. Dusty Miller was No. 2 on Prudent.

11 – Promotion And A Transfer To *HMRT Prudent*

IT WASN'T LONG before we made another trip to St John's, Newfoundland. I was returning to *Restive* one night on foot, passing some railway wagons near the harbour, when I heard the plaintive cries of a kitten. On such a cold night, the kitten really was a pitiful sight. I put it inside my great coat where the warmth seemed to bring it some comfort. This black and white cat made her home in my room. She became a very popular pet throughout the ship, and carried the name Whiskers. Despite having to be rescued from the water twice, she grew into a lovely cat. One day we lay alongside another naval vessel in Reykjavik, which happened to be carrying a very fine tomcat. It was not too long before we discovered our Whiskers was going to become a mother. One dark and stormy night we were south of Iceland, searching for a torpedoed tanker of the British Tanker Company. As 2nd Engineer, I was on the middle watch, 4 to 8 morning and evening. When I eventually got back to my room, I found Whiskers at the foot of my bed with five newly born kittens. Although I had left a suitable box on the floor, she had had them in her favourite spot. I had for

Crew members on HMRT Prudent.

a long time spread a piece of blanket over the bottom of the bed for her, as she used to occasionally get fuel oil on her feet. Many a time I woke up to find kittens asleep all around my head, on my chest and elsewhere. One thing about cats, they are spotlessly clean. How that cat coped in bad weather I just do not know. Eventually the kittens were able to feed themselves, and I managed without any trouble whatsoever to find them homes on other ships. Incidentally, it sticks out in my mind that these kittens were born on Friday the thirteenth.

About this time we returned to the U.K. with a ship in tow. I believe it had gone ashore in the big gale off Reykjavik and had been recovered by the R.N. salvage unit. We handed over our tow in the Clyde to harbour tugs, and we went to Greenock for boiler cleaning and some general repairs after a short spell in Campbeltown. I was told that I had been promoted to chief engineer and that I had been granted leave. I was instructed that on my return to Campbeltown, I was to await passage to the U.S.A. to join one of the new diesel electric rescue tugs, made available under the Lease-Lend Act. After I returned from my parents' home near Colchester, I called in at St Enochs Hotel to see Commander Parker, informing him that

HMRT Prudent.

I intended to spend the last couple of days of my leave in Glasgow. In fact, after discussion it was agreed that I could stay in Glasgow until arrangements for passage to the U.S.A. were finalised. The following afternoon I returned to where I was staying, to find a naval signalman on the doorstep, with a signal instructing me to report "forthwith" to *HMRT Prudent* at Ardrossen. I managed to get there the same evening to find that *Prudent* was ready to sail, but had no chief engineer. Lt. E Martin R.N.R. had reported sick. Rumour had it that word had leaked out that *Prudent* was going a long way away for a very long time. So I joined the crew of *Prudent* on 30th April 1942, and never went to the U.S.A.

The Officers I can remember were the C.O., Lt. Guy Quinn, R.N.R., Sub Lt Russell R.N.R., Sub Lt Ferguson R.N.V.R., 2nd Engineer Sub Lt Pat Murray R.N.V.R., 3rd Engineer, and Sub Lt Tommy Reed R.N.V.R. The senior radio operator was Duncan Reid assisted by someone called "Hayseed".

As we did not sail as soon as anticipated, the following afternoon I took a stroll around Ardrossen. On top of a pile of rubbish in a garden I noticed a very battered child's pedal car. With my own son David in mind, I eventually went back to the house concerned, knocked on the door and offered to buy the 'wreck'. The people concerned were only too pleased to give it to someone who could put it to further use. Not only did I finish up with the pedal car, but also my tea and an interesting chat. Once I had lugged it aboard *Prudent*, I secured it at the top of the engine-room.

We sailed and picked up a convoy coming from the Clyde bound for Gibraltar. It was our understanding that we were to be based there. One Saturday morning soon after our arrival in Gibraltar, we had just finished taking on fuel oil and supplies and were getting ready to go ashore when, without warning, there were explosions from ships anchored in the outer harbour. Air raid sirens were sounded and everything went into an immediate alert routine. We, and all the smaller vessels, were instructed to lie alongside the big naval units, such as battleships, aircraft carriers or cruisers, to offer them some protection against torpedoes. It was later discovered that the Italians had been using two-man submarines. They had been housed in a tanker, especially adapted for the project, with underwater doors. The alert lasted for about 48 hours until it had been established what had happened.

Our first assignment took *Prudent* about 500 miles into the Mediterranean. The U.S. Navy aircraft carrier *Wasp* had conveyed, and was flying off, British fighter aircraft to hard-pressed Malta. On this occasion, our services were not required so we returned to Gibraltar. One morning whilst ashore in town I met an old friend, Captain Rolly Doe of the Royal Engineers. In peacetime he was a farmer on the Essex-Suffolk border. We used to play rugger together around the Colchester, Harwick, Shotley, Ipswich, Norwich area before I went to sea in mid 1935. He was in Gibraltar with a team of army engineers who were lengthening the runway for aircraft on the north side of 'the rock'. The civilian population of Gibraltar had been evacuated soon after the outbreak of war, so Captain Doe and others based there were able to rent some excellent accommodation. We had a very nice meal at his flat, and too much to drink of some strange concoction, which certainly got the better of me!

One evening a party of us from *Prudent* and another rescue tug went ashore to the Embassy Bar, where ratings and other ranks were downstairs, and officers upstairs. We duly got settled around a table upstairs, which gave us a good view of the cabaret being performed. The dancing girls came over the border from La Linea in Spain. With traditional Spanish dresses and castanets, these girls carried out some very spirited dancing with their own brand of music. All Spaniards had to be back across the border by 21.00 hours. The manager of the place came over to our table, and I suddenly found myself being welcomed like a long lost friend. Eventually the story unfolded itself. During the Spanish Civil War he had been injured by bombing and had got to the quayside at, I believe, Valencia. Someone from a ship had seen his plight and got him aboard, where he received first aid attention and was generally taken care of for a few days. He was, for some unknown reason, quite convinced I was "the so kind officer." It certainly was not me. However I decided his friendship was worth retaining and did not therefore disillusion him. The result was a ringside seat and at least one drink on the house each time I went in. This proved to be a beneficial friendship towards the end of the war.

12 – The Strange Story Of The *Lavington Court*

A SIGNAL WAS received all too soon to sail 'forthwith' to a merchant ship in distress, approximately 200 miles north of the Azores. She was the 5,372-ton motor vessel *Lavington Court,* built in 1940 by Harland and Wolff. Under the command of Captain Sutherland, she had been torpedoed on 19th July 1942. *Prudent* had to steam about 1500 miles to the position given. The weather was fine, sea calm and visibility good. We were able to maintain an average speed of a little over 15 knots, so that we arrived in the search area during the morning of the fourth day out. Late afternoon the *Lavington Court* was sighted, and we reached her at dusk. Lt. Quinn decided we would do nothing until dawn. We then cruised slowly round the vessel on what developed into a clear, calm moonlit night.

At about 21.30 hours the C.O. sent a message for me to meet him on the Bridge. Upon arrival he asked me if I believed in ghosts and, after some discussion on this subject, I advised him that I was open minded. The *Lavington Court* had been torpedoed in her stern just forward of the sternpost, so that she had lost her rudder and propeller. Her cruiser type stern containing the crew's quarters was distorted so that it pointed downwards at about 15 to 20 degrees. The after deckhouse was on this section with a gun mounted on top – the barrel of which was pointing down to the sea. The bows of the vessel were pointing roughly to the north-east and, at the time we were discussing ghosts, the moon was fairly high and to the south.

Prudent was circulating the *Lavington Court* in a clockwise direction about half a mile away. As we were approaching the stern of *Lavington Court* the C.O. wanted me to look carefully at the portside of the sloping deckhouse, which was out of the moonlight and under the extended gun platform, which made that area quite dark. As we came round he said, "Now watch carefully Chief and you'll see a moving whitish glow." Sure enough we did. It was very uncanny indeed. After observing the phenomenon another few times, we decided to turn in and 'sleep on it', as we had a 04.00

hours start in the morning. We had been informed that the crew of the *Lavington Court* had been transferred to another ship in the convoy. There was no point in them remaining aboard as their ship had no propeller or rudder. Other good reasons to leave were the possibility of being torpedoed again, or an enemy boarding party looking for information, food or fuel before they sank the vessel.

Just before daylight *Prudent* hoved-to, and the motorboat was launched. The mate took a small party to handle the towrope, and I went to have a look at the engine-room and the damaged aft. It was still dark, but I had a reasonably powerful non-metallic watertight torch. My first job was to go to the engine-room to check whether it was full of water or dry. *Lavington Court* had been struck aft, so if the engine-room was flooded, it would be because the tunnel watertight door was open. There was a hand-operated remote control at the top of the engine room aft, which enabled one to shut this door. Having done that one would get a portable pump aboard as quickly as possible, and pump out the engine-room and probably the boiler-room as well in the case of a steam ship. Fortunately, the tunnel door on *Lavington Court* was closed and the engine room was dry.

When I got to the bottom platform, I found that the bilge water was just about up to the level of the platform. My next job was to set a bilge pump to work. I'd sailed in a similar type of tanker before the war, and so I was familiar with the layout. It wasn't long before I found an electric pump and standby generator suitable for the job. It is very eerie aboard an abandoned ship, particularly when down below. The first hour or so aboard is the worst until one locates and becomes accustomed to all the strange noises. Much depends on the weather. In calm weather there is usually a swell causing some movement to the vessel so that a form of creaking takes place, which is more evident when below in machinery spaces, or a hold. In bad or heavy weather there was the noise of the wind through the various guys and ropes, masts, and derricks, in addition to the sea slamming into the side of the ship, and even breaking across the decks. Much of what happened depended on the state of the distressed vessel. It could be well down by the bow or the stern, or be listing to port or starboard.

When I'd finished in the engine room of the *Lavington Court,* I returned to the deck and saw that the rope party on the forward deck was still busy. After this I went to look at the torpedo damage aft. Dawn had not quite arrived so it was still pretty dark. We had noticed the evening before that there was a navy torpedo boat (ML) mounted on chocks on the after deck. It was secured by two heavy wires attached to deck rings, welded to sections of the deck, which had been strengthened for the purpose. They then passed over the ML, with suitable packing to stop chafing. On the other side, bottle screws were fitted between the wire ends and the deck anchor rings. A ladder was lashed to the side of the ML, and it appeared that the crew had been sleeping in it whilst on passage. There was evidence of a hurried exit, and no wonder – the torpedo had hit very nearly right underneath them. Upon returning to the deck, I decided to undo the bottle screws so that the ML could float free if we struck further trouble, and it could be handy for us as a lifeboat. By this time, another member of the boarding party had joined me. I believe it was one of our wireless operators. Whilst undoing the bottle screws I told him about the 'ghost'. Our next job was to have a look at the stern of the ship, and so we walked along past the aft deckhouse, on the starboard side, and came to an entrance door to the accommodation. It was still fairly dark and my torch was getting somewhat dim. After stepping over the weather step into the passageway, I took only a few steps before tripping over an obstruction. I found myself full length on top of a very dead man. When I got back on my feet, and with the help of my torch, I was able to take stock of the situation. It was obvious this unfortunate gentleman was a sailor on his way to call the next watch, as a large black kettle lay nearby. The sailor had in fact just arrived at the top of the stairs leading down to the crew's accommodation. Other bodies could be seen in the alleyway of the accommodation below. Later information revealed that the ship was torpedoed just before midnight, and that six crew members were missing, believed killed.

The alleyway in which the sailor lay had entrance doors at both port and starboard ends and both doors were painted white. This explained that our 'ghost' was nothing more than the reflection of the moonlight off the white paint. The movement of the 'ghost' was caused by the wave ripples, varying the angles of reflected moonlight. Mystery solved.

After our ghost hunt, we set about standard procedures for preparing a ship for tow. First we had a quick look around all accommodation at deck level and below, where accessible, to see that all portholes and doors were closed. This would prevent more water from entering the ship. From the personal items left around in the mid-ship's accommodation, all hands must have made a very hurried exit. The ship's safe in the chart room had its door open, and was swinging with the movement of the ship. It was standard procedure for secret codebooks and other documents to be dumped over the side in weighted canvas bags, carried for that purpose. The master of the *Lavington Court* would have expected another torpedo to hit him at any moment. For this reason, he would have ordered the crew into the lifeboats as quickly as possible. At this time, most of the merchant ships going south and around the Cape of Good Hope were carrying war supplies to allied forces in North Africa, and the Middle and Far East. These supplies more often than not included explosives in the form of bombs, torpedoes, mines, shells and cordite charges, and vast quantities of machine gun and rifle bullets. A torpedo into a hold containing that type of cargo was not a pleasant prospect.

The rescue tug service had a very strict code, where no looting was allowed. The personal effects around the cabins of an abandoned ship would include wallets, watches, radios and so on. The safe of the *Lavington Court* contained quite a considerable sum of money in various currencies, so we simply relocked the door. This would ensure a degree of safety if we got the ship to port and rope-handling people came aboard. Locking cabin doors was also a good idea if keys were available. The keys would be hidden, and someone in authority at the port of arrival would be advised accordingly. The steward's pantry with the ship's cutlery was always popular with looters.

Making fast the wire tow ropes to a ship was a difficult task, particularly in this case when a long tow to Falmouth or the Bristol Channel was anticipated. Anti-chafe measures had to be taken at all points where the towing wires come in contact with steel. Suitable pieces of timber were used, and lashed around bollards and such like. The load and stress on these wires would of course be considerable in adverse weather. Where the wires actually left the bows of the ship, they would dip downwards to follow the curvature of the sag in the towing rope, which could have been 1800 to 2000 feet long, with a total weight of around 8 to 10 tons. At the point of dip, timbers such as cargo hatch boards were lashed to the wire, and anything that moved was well greased.

By the time we were ready to leave the *Lavington Court,* we had been there about 2½ hours. During that time our motor lifeboat had been assisting *Prudent* with the towing wires. Standard procedure would be to connect the 18 inch manila tow rope, all of which is very scientifically laid out on the tug's aft deck, in such a way that both wire and manila rope are free to uncoil as they run out over the tug's stern. As soon as the ropes are fully out, the towing load will be very gently taken up. Next a bridle or gob-rope will be made fast at one end to a gobbing bollard, passed through the gob eye, and then over the towrope, back through the gob eye and then made fast to the gobbing bollard. This rope or bridle contains the towrope so that it can only pass over the stern of the tug, and will reduce the movement of the towrope so that it cannot get over the side of the tug, and possibly foul the propeller. It also cuts down the movement of the towrope and helps to reduce chafing at the after bulwark surface. A large board is usually tied to the rope so that the board rides on the bulwark railing, assisted by plenty of grease. Between the aft bulwark and the towing hook is what are generally known as towing arches, which keep the towing rope clear of all the aft deck obstructions, such as the engine room casing and skylights, salvage and fire pump connections, capstan, bollards and so on. These arches are greased and boards will be fixed under the towrope so that friction can be reduced.

When all preparations had been made for towing, two people were left aboard the casualty, and the motorboat returned to the tug. The motorboat then had to be swung onboard *Prudent*, and secured. How this was done depended on weather conditions. Getting the motorboat back aboard was not too difficult that day, as the weather was reasonable. The motorboat approached the tug from astern, and came on ahead until the tug crew could get hold of the lifeboat falls. At a suitable moment the order to heave up was given, and the boat was quickly raised to the davit head, winched aboard, and re-stowed.

At this stage the serious business of towing could get underway, and a course was worked out to the nearest port. In the case of the *Lavington Court*, it was desirable to keep well away from the Bay of Biscay and the French coast. Everything went fine until about the third day. We decided to go aboard again, to check the towing gear and the bilge water in the engine room and elsewhere. At this time we were having gauge glass problems on the boiler of *Prudent*, and I had hoped to obtain some spare parts from the service boiler on *Lavington Court*. This service boiler supplies steam to the ship's domestic services and some pumps in the engine room. At sea, the exhaust from the main engine – a six cylinder Burmister and Wain Diesel about 35 feet high – would maintain steam, assisted by an oil burner. These waste heat boilers would be run entirely on oil in port. Whilst carrying out these duties, a corvette arrived for escort duties. We had a large armed trawler with us, but she needed to proceed to port to refuel. After an exchange of visual signals with *Prudent*, who was still towing, the corvette put down a boat and her No.1 and a small party came over to *Lavington Court* to see if replenishments for their rundown food stocks could be obtained. We were able to assist them in this matter as the meat, vegetable and handling rooms were still very cold. I do remember they did very well with tinned turkey. Whilst this transfer of goods was going on, we were chatting with their No.1 who advised us that they had seen a German condor reconnaissance aircraft just before they had sighted us. This was bad news indeed because it meant the Germans would now be aware of the rescue attempt being carried out. Eventually we returned to *Prudent*, who was still towing at around four knots. We were able to render repairs to one of our boiler gauge glasses with a makeshift part from the waste heat boiler.

Around 20.40 hours that night I was in my room making up my log book whilst events were still fresh in my mind, when there was an awful bang as though someone had hit the bottom of *Prudent* with an oversized sledge-hammer. I rushed up to the boat deck and was in time to see the stern of *Lavington Court* disappear under the sea, and her bow lifting up into the air until the ship was vertical. The whole ship then slid down under the waves, surrounded by foaming water. Then all was quiet – very deadly quiet.

Fortunately for us, our towrope had been released. It was a sad sight, and I found during discussions with other crew members from the C.O's downwards, that pretty well everyone was affected emotionally. I have seen a few ships large and small go to their watery graves, and always felt it was like attending the funeral of a relative or friend. As this one was slipping away in the moonlight, I thought of all the skill of design and building that had gone into it. A nearly new ship with lovely accommodation, that in peacetime would have been a great pleasure to work and sail in. What a terrible waste.

Just as *Lavington Court* was disappearing below the waves, we heard the sound of gunfire. The U-boat that had effected the coup de grace had apparently been spotted on the surface by the escort. Our alarm bell went, and the 3 inch guns went into action firing, along with the escort, at a point where gun flashes could be seen. This little exchange went on for about ten minutes, during which time I was in the wheelhouse. The C.O. decided to get away as it was becoming a little vague as to who was firing at whom. I should explain that another rescue tug – I believe *Tenacity* – and an escort had turned up that evening just before dusk, and were cruising around awaiting daylight. We were to receive a topping up of fuel oil from the other tug, before she connected up to the tow to help speed up the operation.

At daylight, Lt. Quinn decided we would return to the area of action the night before and ascertain whether or not the motor launch was afloat. Very soon it was located afloat and in good order and taken in tow on a 4.5 inch wire rope, or pennant, approximately 90 fathoms long. After a couple of days towing we were instructed to proceed to Milford Haven. At daylight on the morning we were due in Milford Haven, it was discovered that the motor launch was under water at her bow. Towing stopped, the wire was hauled in and the ML brought alongside. We were able to see with the rise and fall of its bows, that one porthole had opened. We put this down to the rough weather, which could have caused enough vibration for the brass thumbscrews to come undone. We connected up a few lengths of our 7 inch suction hoses so that with our main stream salvage and fire pump, we were able to quickly reduce the water level in the forward part of the ML.

After swimming a short distance under water, I managed to get in and close and secure the offending porthole. We didn't have far to go before we arrived at our anchorage. Just before arriving there another ML came out and took charge of our tow. After dark that night, possibly just around midnight, our alarm bells went off indicating an air raid. I popped up to the bridge to see what was happening. One or two of the others had already arrived there to man the guns on the bridge wings. The 2nd mate was concentrating on a point in the sky possibly 3 or 4 miles to the east, where 3 search light beams were holding steady on a spot high in the sky. We could hear the up-and-down note of a German aircraft, and then the higher note of another – which we took to be a British night fighter. Soon there was gunfire far above followed by an aircraft bursting into flames. Down it came in a rather erratic round and round, up and down sort of way, until finally it crashed about 3 miles away on, or near, a beach. There were some heavy explosions followed by a 'firework' display of various colours and ascending bullets, all being activated by the very hot fire fanned by the night breeze, and fed by a few hundred gallons of aviator spirit. I learned in later years that the German was shot down by an English night fighter pilot, who later became a well-known test pilot.

13 – More Rail Travel In War Time Britain

THE NEXT MORNING we went alongside the long fish quay in Milford Haven, which was near the main dock entrance. We took aboard a new 18 inch circumference tow rope which was 120 fathoms long, and two 90 fathom towing wires. The powers-that-be decided we should have a boiler clean and also quite a lot of work done on the bridge and wireless room. We all got leave in turn and I went to Glasgow. What an awful journey it was in wartime! Upon arrival at Crewe there was a long delay from something like mid evening until 03.00 hours. The station was fairly crowded with service personnel of many nationalities, mostly sitting in groups, talking and smoking. A few groups were carrying their own booze, and were quite noisy. There was often singing. I can remember some Polish gentlemen giving quite an impressive impromptu choral concert. All this was taking place on the platforms of an almost blacked out station. A seemingly endless number of southbound trains were passing through the station, hour after hour. These troop trains passed through the station quite slowly, with a number of Americans hanging out of each open window. As soon as one train had gone, another would appear within about ten minutes. My interest in railway engines was well satisfied that night! What a job it must have been for the railway personnel to organise movements like this when a troop convoy arrived, in this case in the Clyde. As usual, I was full of admiration for those idols of my childhood – the driver and the fireman of those fine steam railway engines. What problems they would have on a night like this. I have often wondered in recent years what would have happened had the 'Industrial Saboteurs' of today, 1979, been around in wartime.

Those troop trains were the cause of our delay that night. We did eventually reach Glasgow on a very long and overcrowded train from London. Fortunately I had a first class warrant and found a seat and managed some very troubled sleep. An overcrowded train in those days consisted mainly of forces personnel going on leave or returning to their units. They always had a well packed kit bag with other odd items of equipment, and of course we all had to carry a service gas mask and tin hat. Those who could not find a space in a compartment would establish themselves in the corridor and sit on their gear. Movement to and from the toilets was quite some problem. Civilian travellers intermingling with this lot had their problems too.

When going on leave one had to bear in mind the restrictions of food rationing. Being at sea most of the time, it was possible for us to pick up useful tinned items such as meat, fruit, coffee, tea, jam, butter and fish. A wise man would know the silk stocking sizes for the lady folk in his family or his girl-friend, or girl-friends! It was amazing when one looks back how the folks at home did manage on their ration cards. Other acceptable presents that come to mind were cigarettes, biscuits and sweets.

After three days in Glasgow I had to face the tedious journey back to Milford Haven. For some reason or other I could not get further than Cardiff that night. I booked into a hotel and after something to eat went to the bar. Immediately upon arrival there, two ladies walked over to me and one offered her hand, and from the corner of her mouth said "We're Navy wives, please rescue us from those Yanks." It appeared three reasonably pleasant American army officers were trying to chat up these women on their own in a bar. These two ladies were mother and daughter and they had lost their husbands when *H.M.S. Prince of Wales* and *H.M.S. Repulse* were sunk by Japanese aircraft on 10th December 1941. Both men were regular R.N. engine room artificers. Having discussed our common problems I saw them safely home in the blackout, and that was that.

Arrival back at *Prudent* revealed that our new C.O. was Lt. Kenneth Atkinson R.N.R., a Liverpool man. One of the first jobs when returning from leave was to get the engine-room logbook up to date. All work carried out, either by dockyard or engine-room personnel, was recorded. At sea the logbook was completed at midday as soon as fuel tank and boiler fresh water tank soundings were known. Other important items in the logbook were hours run by the various items of machinery, so that preventive maintenance could be carried out when the appropriate number of running hours had been reached. In the case of boilers, steaming hours were recorded.

One personal problem was to send the pedal-car I picked up in Ardrossen to my son David. I had rebuilt it whilst at sea. One of the carpenters working aboard *Prudent* produced a very nice packing case for a few bottles of whisky. Before finally sealing up the box to travel by mail, I got a customs officer from the dockyard gate nearby to inspect the case before screwing down the lid. We toasted the box and the pedal-car and a happy customs officer declared all was well. However, I did manage to pop in a few odd items of use to my parents before the box went to the station on a borrowed fish barrow. Some weeks later I got word from my parents in Colchester that the whole lot had arrived intact.

When preparing to go on a trip of unknown duration all stores are topped up. The mate or No.1 was responsible for all deck stores such as ropes, paints and lifeboat equipment. The 2nd mate got the navigational charts likely to be required, and saw that all charts were brought up to date, using current signals and correspondence. The C.O. and wireless personnel would have secret codes to deal with. Food was taken care of by the chief steward in consultation with the C.O. and the cook. Engine room stores, fuel oil and boiler feed water were more usually a combined effort by the chief and 2nd engineer, with the 3rd engineer looking after electrical spares – or the electrician where one was carried, such as on the diesel electric tugs. Ammunition for the guns was usually taken care of by the 2nd mate with the advice and assistance of the gunner. And so by team work the whole ship was made ready for sea. The odd meeting was held by those responsible for the different departments with the C.O. so that he, who had overall responsibility, was satisfied that everything was in order to set sail.

14 – Gibraltar, Freetown And Crossing The Equator

WE WERE INSTRUCTED to escort about a dozen Motor Launches from the Bristol Channel to Gibraltar, and to take in tow any that broke down. The usual course well out into the Atlantic was followed to about 27 degrees west, and then south until a point was reached to make a turn east to Gibraltar. During the second day out we ran into some really bad weather, which stayed with us for about three days. Standing on the bridge of *Prudent* was an education of what happens to small ships in big seas. The waves were around 20 to 30 feet and *Prudent* was far from comfortable. One could look around one moment, and not a single ML was in sight. Then suddenly one would appear on a wave crest climbing at what appeared to be an angle of anything up to 45 degrees, and then level up and take a dive the into next wave trough. It was amazing how man and boat could survive and maintain station. Fortunately we did run into reasonable weather, and there came a stage where they were able to open up and make Gibraltar a few hours earlier than expected. As far as I remember we had one in tow on arrival.

Gibraltar was as usual a hive of activity with major naval units, submarines and other smaller vessels coming and going for repairs, stores, fuel and so on. There were some quite hectic scenes ashore some nights. There was little to do other than to visit the bars. Sometimes there were concerts, or the cinema, and notices advising amenities ashore were usually posted on the ship's notice board upon arrival in port. A notice would also advise what and where was out of bounds, and other hazards to avoid. The civilian population of Gibraltar had been evacuated, so that those individuals who sought the company of ladies would have to cross over into La Linea in Spain, but passes for this purpose were limited I believe. We used to find that in places like Gibraltar, where there were only a few service women, and maybe a few hundred, or a few thousand service men, it was extremely difficult to make a date unless you had a friend or a relative amongst the girls.

During this spell of two or three days in Gibraltar, I contacted my army friend Rolly, who took me along to see the work they were doing extending the runway. By this time I believe one or two large aircraft had run over the end of the runway and disappeared into the water. There they were buried under the extended runway. We also received the unjustified hospitality of the Embassy Bar. After two or three days we did another mystery trip into the Med in order to be on hand if required. There were other rescue tugs based at Gibraltar. I believe *HMRT Salvonia* was there under Lt Peter McCabe R.N.R. After two or three days in the Med we returned to Gibraltar, and within two days we sailed with *Salvonia* to Freetown, Sierra Leone.

From Gibraltar onwards, we found *Prudent* was becoming a very warm ship once we got into the tropics. It was August 1942. *Prudent* and *Restive* had five steam-heated systems designed for arctic waters. Nothing on the ship was designed to keep us cool. The use of canvas deck awning was rather limited on this class of rescue tug, but it was possible to have some either side of the accommodation on the boat deck and in front of the bridge over the fore deck. Lying at anchor in Freetown was indeed a very warm business, and you could not just hop over the ship's side for a swim and cool off because of sharks.

We used our own motorboat as a duty boat for shore leave. The rather crude landing stage was known as King Tom, and from there one could walk into Freetown. On the way there was a bridge over a fresh water stream where the local ladies could be seen doing their laundry by rinsing the clothes in the water and banging them on a suitable rock. The main attraction here was the fact that the local ladies were 'topless'. Although common place these days, the sight of half naked women was a new experience for young sailors in the 1940's. But after a day or two the novelty of someone else's way of life wears off, and conversations return to normal.

Talking of conversations, one could always hear the odd conversation going on around a ship when lying at anchor when all was quiet. In hot weather small groups would sit about in shady spots and discuss just about everything under the sun. On the

Assurance Class tug there were two stokehold ventilators which terminated just above and at the back of the bridge accommodation. When someone was facing these ventilator tops, they could hear very clearly a conversation going on below. Usually the stoker or watch would sit under the ventilator to keep cool, and from time to time would be joined by the duty greaser from the engine-room.

Freetown was a very important port in wartime and a hive of activity with all classes of naval ships coming and going. Convoys for merchant ships were formed there too. The South Atlantic H.Q. was based there on the old Union Castle liner *Edinburgh Castle*. *H.M.S. Vindictive* had been converted into a repair ship. There was also a small Fleet Air Arm base, *H.M.S. Hastings*. When thinking of Freetown I always remember, both in peacetime and wartime, the native hum-boats. The locals would hang around ships in canoes, diving for coins, and offering fruit, monkeys and many other goods for sale. Swimming could be enjoyed at Lumley Beach, where a reef protects the beach area from sharks.

On the second day there, after we had finished taking fuel, water and stores, three or four of us decided to take a stroll ashore in the morning, and to visit an officers' club we had heard about. When we arrived at this club we found it was a very makeshift affair and one literally sat on orange boxes. However there was a very cheerful atmosphere and reasonable drink at duty free prices. I got a very pleasant surprise when my old friend Ted Noble walked in. He had been the first mate on *Restive* during our early days in the North Atlantic and Iceland. Around June 1942 he left *Restive* with a chest complaint, and left the rescue tug service soon after that. It was interesting to discover that he had become the captain of a local tug. After much talking and many tots, we went back to Ted's boat, calling at *Prudent* first so that they could find me if an emergency arose. It was an older type coal burning steam tug, with a crew of about every nationality – they looked like a bunch of pirates! Ted, although a pleasant rather easygoing character, knew how to handle this lot, and they all seemed to treat him with the greatest of respect. After a rather wild drinking session, I was eventually taken back to *Prudent*, and woke up the following morning the proud possessor of a mongoose and a large coloured umbrella. I suddenly remembered that Ted's tug was something of a menagerie with parrots, a dog or two and some weird looking creatures kept by crew members in cages. This mongoose became quite a pet and carried the name Mongie. We had a dog onboard at that time called Scouse, who had been taken off an abandoned ship in the North Atlantic before I joined *Prudent*. He was a real ship's dog of a friendly disposition, and well looked after by all the crew. He and the mongoose became quite good friends. The coloured umbrella was of the type carried by all and sundry in Freetown, for the simple reason you can be walking along with the sun 'splitting the heavens' in a blue sky, and without warning a sudden tropical storm lets loose a deluge of rain for ten minutes or so.

During our short spell in Freetown we were alerted to proceed to a troop ship, which had been torpedoed not far away. However we had not gone far when we were recalled as news had been received that the ship in question had sunk, and the survivors had been picked up. After the war I discovered an old friend of mine had been on the ship. She had just joined the Army as a nursing sister, and was on her way to her first assignment in the Middle East. She landed in Freetown the worse for a ducking in heavy fuel oil and seawater. All her new uniforms had gone to the bottom of the sea.

We finally left Freetown with a Dutch submarine, and instructions to escort it to Simonstown, South Africa. Our overall escort was a Corvette manned by a Free French crew. The submarine required a major repair on the port clutch between the port diesel engine and generator. We met the Dutch C.O. of the submarine before leaving Freetown. He was a man of medium build with gingerish hair and full beard – in fact he really looked the part. They had had quite a successful time in the Mediterranean and their last sinking was a U-boat. The C.O. did advise us he would occasionally carry out diving and gunnery exercises. His submarine was fully operational but not capable of full speed on the surface. Our first stop was to be Pointe Novie in the (then) French Congo.

The first time the submarine C.O. advised that they would carry out diving exercises we all got to vantage points to watch. During the whole trip, the submarine maintained station about 150 yards in line on our starboard side. The escorting Corvette was a little further away on the same quarter. When diving time arrived, the submarine was gone in a matter of seconds. Shortly afterwards the small attacking periscope could be seen protruding about a foot or so above the surface, leaving a faint wash behind. The sea was slightly choppy at the time and we could only really watch this periscope because we knew exactly where to look. What an impossible thing to spot at sea in the normal run of things. It had been pre-arranged that our C.O. would press the alarm bell button when the submarine surfaced, to give our gun crews some drill practice. The submarine quickly popped up, with a flurry of white foam. Even before all the spray and foam had subsided, their gun crews were at their stations. This was seconds before our C.O. could press the alarm bell, which was only just above his right shoulder. When we discussed this incident afterwards, we found it hard to believe the speed of what we had witnessed. It did certainly prove what we had heard about the extremely high standard of training maintained in the submarine service. We were to see this exercise performed another few times, still completely fascinated by the speed of the whole operation. It was also good training for our crew. Although most of them had had some gunnery training at Campbeltown, they had to rely upon the one fully trained gunner we carried for further training. The gunner was also responsible for keeping all the guns in good working order. However, his main job was the three-inch gun, which could be used for surface or anti-aircraft work.

Only a limited amount of stores where available at Pointe Novie, but we did pick up plenty of fruit and vegetables and some meat. Before reaching this port however, we had crossed the equator, which meant that a 'crossing-the-line-ceremony' had to be arranged to initiate the first timers. We had a tarpaulin tied up by its four corners on the after deck, and a hatch board was arranged to carry a chair. The victim sat in the chair, was well lathered with shaving soap, and a wooden razor of large proportions was brought into use by Father Neptune and his assistants, all suitably dressed. After or during the shaving session, the victim was tipped over backwards into the water, and after a good ducking was considered initiated. It was surprising how the crew rose to an occasion like this and produced the most amazing homemade props.

The C.O. and I had occasion to go aboard the corvette one evening. Although we did have a good reason to be there, the French crew did not seem very pleased to see us. We later came to the conclusion they were on our side, but only just! There was an English lieutenant R.N.V.R. with them, carrying out the duties of liaison officer. All business was carried out with him acting as interpreter.

15 – South Africa And Our New Base – Durban

WE LEFT POINTE Novie that night, as it had been decided that we should 'slip away in the dark'. We had a journey of 2,250 miles to Simonstown, which passed without any undue event. The days were very hot and the sea calm and so the time passed quite quickly. When approaching the Cape we received instructions to go into Saldanha Bay, which was about 75 miles north of Cape Town. This bay had a rather narrow entrance and was therefore reasonably easy to defend. Ships were being directed in there because mines had recently been laid by the enemy off the Cape. A number of ships had been damaged and sunk off the Cape by mines since late 1941.

Our old friend *H.M.S. Hecla* was at anchor in Saldanha Bay, and the Dutch submarine was instructed to tie up alongside her. We anchored not very far from a wooden jetty at the head of the bay. During the afternoon we put down the motorboat and a party went ashore to get some exercise and have a general look round. In the early evening a party from the wardroom went ashore including the mate, the wireless operator, the 3rd engineer and myself. The place was a small holiday resort made up mainly of wooden bungalows. There was one little bar with a small dance floor. After a longish walk we reached the bar and spent the evening there. The mate, we had already discovered, could become something of a problem when he was drunk. That night was no exception, and we had a job to get him down to the jetty and into the motorboat. We then discovered he had lost his hat. I had a look along the dusty excuse for a road we had taken from the bar, which was only a matter of three or four minutes walk, but could not see the hat anywhere. I returned to the jetty to find the boat had gone off without me! The next morning I was told that the mate had insisted upon a trip around the harbour but had soon fallen asleep and was promptly taken back aboard *Prudent* and put to bed. By this time I had been forgotten. When I discovered the motorboat had gone, I naturally thought they would come back for me, so returned to the bar to wait for them. After about ten minutes a man and two ladies walked in, carrying a naval officer's hat. They had picked it up nearby whilst out for a stroll. We finished up having quite a party and eventually I was returned to *Prudent* in their motorboat. The people concerned were from Cape Town and were staying at their own holiday bungalow. They were going home in a couple of days and I was invited to call on them if I ever visited Cape Town.

The following day the C.O. and I were invited to *Hecla* for gin at 11.30 hours. Also among the guests were the C.O.'s of the French corvette and the Dutch submarine, with some of their officers. At the end of this gathering I made enquires to see if the gentleman from Glasgow was still in charge of the N.A.A.F. stores. He was and I was taken down to his cabin, which seemed to be in the very bowels of *Hecla*. He was pleased to see me and a bottle of the very best Scotch was produced. What with the gin in the wardroom and this whisky below deck, I have only a vague memory of getting to the Dutch submarine which was the next port of call. I remember going down to the lower control room of the submarine and bending down to pass through a small opening into the wardroom. From accounts afterwards it appeared I did not bend low enough and cracked my head on the top edge of this opening. That was my last memory of the submarine. When I finally came to, I was in my own bunk with a bandage round my head!

During the early morning hours of darkness, we sailed for Simonstown with the submarine. As we were approaching Simonstown at dusk, a warning shot was fired across our bows from the shore. Apparently someone had not been told that a submarine would be following us. Simonstown had a very fine harbour with much naval tradition evident in the solid way the harbour walls, dry docks and shore establishments were built. The scenery was very attractive looking across False Bay. Table Mountain could be seen, as well as the sandy beaches of the small seaside resorts around Table Bay. A very efficient electric railway of 3 feet 6 inch gauge ran the 36 miles between Simonstown and Cape Town. This railway ran along the coast through Musenberg, Wynberg, Salt River, and Stellenbosch, to name but a few of its 36 stations. From

False Bay it ran across the Cape Peninsula to Cape Town on Table Bay.

Prudent was instructed to proceed to Cape Town to have air trunking and fans fitted to keep the accommodation cool. This installation, boiler cleaning, and other jobs would take about three weeks. As a result of this, everyone had the chance of some leave, and an opportunity to explore the Cape. The weather was becoming very warm as mid-summer down there is around Christmas time. I was unable to spend much time away from the ship as I had to supervise some of the installations. I was able to make short trips and the people I had met in Saldanha Bay showed me round many places of interest. I met a detective sergeant in the South African police force who invited me to his home, and I used to stay there occasionally. The people of Cape Town were very generous and hospitable, and all hands enjoyed their stay there. However, the walk back to the dockyard could be tricky as mugging, as it's now called, was not unheard of.

But to be fair to Cape Town, the pastime of robbing sailors returning to their ships has gone on for generations throughout the world – except in Japan in my experience. One of the charge-hands working on *Prudent* in Cape Town told the story of the very fit Commander R.N. who was returning from a long walk one evening, and was attacked by four muggers. He beat the lot up to the extent that they had to receive hospital treatment! After the work in Cape Town was finished, we returned to Simonstown for a short spell. Personally I would have been very happy to stay in the Cape. The main station at Cape Town was always of interest and I got to know people at the Salt River running sheds. Although it was just a narrow gauge railway, the South Africans had some mighty big engines.

We left Simonstown to join a convoy going north, with a stop at Durban. At that time we were still under the impression that we were going to the eastern end of the Mediterranean. We duly arrived at Durban and tied up at Maydon Wharf on a Thursday afternoon. The usual instructions came aboard from the local naval base, which was in a requisitioned newspaper office in West Street. The actual naval stores were contained in three large garages. South African naval personnel were very evident here. The two engineer officers in charge of repairs were both English, but actually in the South African Navy. In peace time one of them had been an agent for Crossley Engines. The second officer was Lt. Commander E. Coward, who had been a merchant service engineer and had settled in South Africa pre-war.

When we needed to travel to the naval stores, we telephoned their transport department and a car was sent to the ship. The drivers were volunteers and Durban ladies of some standing. On my second day in Durban I did this, and my driver was a Mrs Sexton, who mentioned before we parted that she was having a little party at her home that evening and extended an invitation. What a magnificent house! It was up on the Beira overlooking the whole of Durban, built in a Spanish style. Mr Sam Sexton was a very successful bookmaker. When leaving that night one received the usual invitation, "to be sure and let us know if you come back to Durban".

The following day, a Saturday, we were taking on fuel oil at the south side of the harbour when an urgent signal was received to proceed forthwith to a Harrison ship which had been torpedoed about 150 miles off Durban. Two days later we found the ship drifting with the crew still aboard. They had been hit in the stern, and had lost both rudder and propeller. With their own crew they were able to make fast the towropes, and we were soon underway in calm weather. About a week later we arrived back at Durban where our tow was taken over by two of the large railway harbour tugs that they had there. As soon as we had taken in and stowed our towing gear we entered the harbour and went for fuel oil, and then to No.1 berth Maydon Wharf. The C.O. went ashore to H.Q. and came back with the news that we were to be based in Durban. I remember at lunch we discussed this news with mixed feelings because we rather felt we were out of the war. However, as it turned out there was a busy life ahead for us from the Cape through the

Mozambique Channel to the Gulf of Aden. At this time troop and supply convoys going to North Africa, the Middle East and India, were calling at Durban. Ships returning to the U.K. were taking back foodstuffs, oil and so on. The convoy system required escort ships so that Simonstown, Durban, Mombasa and Aden became important naval bases.

Durban was not only a major port, but also one of the leading holiday resorts in South Africa. The amazing thing was that these two aspects of Durban did not clash. The sea front had its gardens, lawns, a model railway, some first class hotels, and you could even get your photo taken with a Zulu warrior in full regalia. In the very hot summer period from around October to March, people would spend the whole day at the sea front. Bathing was behind safety nets to keep out the sharks. At the time we were based in Durban, the Edward hotel was 'the' hotel. The lounge had palm trees, Indian waiters and a Grand Hotel type orchestra playing in the evenings – it was a place where people liked to be seen. The sea front was to the north side at the Cumberland Hotel and was owned by Mr and Mrs Isaacs. A little further on were the country club and the local aerodrome. The southern end of the sea front ended at the port entrance, alongside the main docks. On the opposite side of the port entrance was a spit of land known as the Bluff, extending out to sea forming a good protection for shipping entering and leaving the port. On the Bluff there was a whale processing factory, complete with its own whaling vessels.

Maydon Wharf was around a mile long, with a wide quayside backed by large storage accommodation for complete cargoes. Opposite No.1 Maydon Wharf was an extensive timber yard. At the other end of the Wharf was a flying boat base at Congella, along with some dry docks. This flying boat service was to a lake near Johannesburg, and operated by four-engined Shorts flying boats. They took off and landed alongside Maydon Wharf.

One of the first jobs for *Prudent* was target towing. These sea going targets were referred to as 'Epping Forest' because of the amount of timber used to build them. The hull was usually about

30 feet long by 6 or 8 feet wide, with a deep draught of around 15 feet. They had a weighted keel to keep them as upright as possible at sea. On the deck were towing bollards and wood lattice work, approximately 30 feet long by 30 feet high, with various metal contraptions at the top so that they could be picked up on radar by exercising ships.

These target practices usually took place fifteen or twenty miles off shore, day or night. The target would be towed on full towing gear at full speed, which would be about 15 knots in reasonable weather. The wireless operators would advise the C.O. when shooting was to take place, as we were at action stations in case the rescue tug was hit. The Brigand Class rescue tug *Buccaneer (W.49)* was lost in this way on 25th August 1946. One could first hear and then see these shells as they approached the target. The first launch of shells usually went a little over the target, the next lot just short, and the next and following shots would straddle the target. On two occasions *Prudent* was straddled by shells when a warship's radar got on to the wrong target. An urgent wireless message went off post haste before the next salvo was on its way! There was an old cruiser based in Durban which was used by various navel units to practice their gunnery skills.

After a month or two in Durban most of the crew, including Scouse the ship's dog, had made friends with some of the locals. I was lucky that the Sextons 'adopted' me, and allowed me the use of a very comfortable bedroom, and a front door key. I was also given the key to a Vauxhall car, and told to come and go as I wished. The car part of it worried me because we got invited to some rather hectic parties as time went on. This little problem was solved when I was in a car breakers' yard one day, looking for some bits-and-pieces for the Gray Marine petrol engine fitted to our motorboat. The owner was originally from near Hampton Court, which I knew well as a child as my mother came from this area. I mention this because if you are abroad and establish a common link with someone, they welcome you as if you were a long lost relative. This friendship enabled me to purchase at a very reasonable price an

Austin Seven of early 1930's vintage. I drove it back to *Prudent* the day before we were to depart with a convoy for Mombasa. A considerable amount of work had to be done to recondition the Austin, so it was winched onboard the boat deck and lashed down near the 3 inch gun. The car had an overhaul second to none, with everything stripped back. Fortunately the Austin Seven is a very simple car and we were able to adapt or make things such as door and bonnet fittings. By the time we got back to Durban it ran like a new car. It used to stand on the quay by the wood yard fence at Maydon Wharf.

When we first arrived in Mombasa we tied up at a buoy in Kilindini Harbour, alongside one of the 'Epping Forest' targets. Fuel oil was taken from a Royal Fleet Auxiliary tanker, and stores were ordered and collected ashore. Mombasa was an interesting town and port where Africa, the Middle East and the Far East met. The old port of Mombasa was to the north of the town, which had the ancient Fort Jesus, where Arab dhows still traded alongside small modern vessels and fishing boats. All the big shipping went into Kilindini, as it had large safe anchorage and modern jetties. I was greatly interested in the large Garrett railway locomotives being unshipped there and assembled on the quayside. They were built by the North British Locomotive Company, shipped out in three sections and assembled on the quay. I got to know the engineer in charge who had been a seafarer and had settled out there pre-war. He arranged little rides for us on these engines from time to time. On more than one occasion the 2nd engineer Pat Murray and I used to drive and stoke one of the tank locos shunting on the quays at night. A packet of cigarettes worked wonders with the native driver and fireman, not forgetting the gentleman in charge of shunting.

Nightlife in Mombasa as far as we were concerned was the Officers' Club, the Merchant Navy Club and the Women's Service Club. The point in moving around the three clubs was the fact that decent beer and spirits were rationed. After we had partaken of our ration in the Officers' Club, we would move on to the Merchant

Navy Club, after leaving signs of our Royal Navy uniform such as epaulettes and caps at the Officers' Club. We were of course, still on merchant service articles under T124T admiralty agreement. I remember on one occasion being invited aboard a ship one night, on my way back to Kilindini, by an engineer. They were loading mules, mule carts and Indian troops for India. Looking down into the hold, I could see that the heavy equipment had been loaded in the bottom, the mules in stalls on the next level and above that the troops on special tiers of bunks. Two things struck me right away – how did they stick the smell and the heat, and what would the confusion be like in the event of the ship being torpedoed?

Our first trip out at Mombasa was target towing, which was not our favourite pastime. More interesting was our exploration of the local area. To the north of Mombasa is a pontoon bridge carrying the road running north to Malindi. We were lucky enough to discover Banburi, or White Sands holiday camp, run by a Mr and Mrs Crosslands. The accommodation was in the form of a number of native type chalets, with a large central building where the owners lived, containing the dining and recreation area. The chalets were dotted about under palm trees, next to miles of beautiful sandy beaches. At low tide one could get out to a coral reef where a wide variety of exotic small marine life could be seen in the pools and crevasses. It really was a delightful spot to get away from it all. Members of the other services found their way there too – particularly from bases inland.

We did quite a lot of target towing during our first spell in Mombasa, but we were always 'on station' for emergency calls. At this time German U-boats came around the Cape and up the east coast of Africa as far as Aden. We got to know when one was about by the fact that our readiness notices would drop, say, from 4 hours to 2 hours to immediate notice. This applied in both Durban and Mombasa. There was also, we discovered later, the odd Japanese and Italian submarine operating on this coast. One afternoon in Kilindini the air raid warning siren went off and all ships and shore establishments had to stand to action station. Anti-aircraft shooting produced the usual puffs of smoke high in the sky where we could see the mere speck of an aircraft. Eventually we discovered this was a reconnaissance Japanese seaplane working from one of three large Japanese submarines of about 3,000 tons, designed to carry aircraft or miniature submarines. These large submarines were responsible for two man submarine operations in southern Australia, Diego Suanez and the West coast of the U.S.A.

Our first emergency call took us south of Mombasa to one of the lease-lend American tugs towing a large floating crane. The tug had broken down and needed a tow to Kilindini. When we returned for the crane, a small party was put aboard to make fast the towing gear – a job made more difficult by the fairly heavy seas running at the time. Unfortunately, one wire rope snapped, and the fixed end whipped round and broke the leg of a sailor. The crane was eventually delivered to Kilindini. The injured sailor was replaced by an interesting chap from the South African Navy, who collected rare timber and was an expert on furniture making. We eventually returned to Durban for boiler cleaning. This enabled most people to get some leave. Many South African families offered leave facilities, which were advertised through the amenities section at the naval base. I preferred to stay by the ship and do the odd daily trip to places of interest, such as the Valley of a Thousand Hills, Port Shepstone, Pietermaritzburg and the well-known bathing beaches north and south of Durban. The railways around Durban were of great interest to me. Local trains were handled in the main by small Garrett type locos, designed for the mountainous conditions west and south of Durban. Mention must be made of the night clubs well known to all passing through Durban – the 'Stardust', the 'Cosmo' and the 'Athlone Gardens'. The latter also served afternoon tea in gardens containing quite a collection of monkeys, who were the world's biggest scroungers.

16 – Saving The *Sheaf Crown* And An Incident Of Looting

THE NEXT TORPEDOED ship we had to locate and assist was about 200 miles off East London. It was the *Sheaf Crown* of 4,800 tons and bound for North Africa. When we sighted it, a white vapour was coming from just forward of the funnel. At first we imagined this was an indication that there was a fire in the stokehold. Closer inspection revealed that the ship had been torpedoed in the No.1 hold on the port side. When we got aboard, I went with a fireman and greaser in the hope that we might be able to raise steam on possibly one of the boilers. Fortunately the boiler room and engine room were quite dry. Before we left *Prudent* it had been decided to tow the *Sheaf Crown* stern first. The rope party made towing wires fast to the stern bollards, with all the usual anti-chafing boards and generous applications of grease. This enabled towing to get underway whilst we made further investigations in the boiler room. The white vapour we saw earlier was actually caused by unlit oil vaporising in the hot furnace. It appeared the stokehold had been abandoned and a fire or two left burning at low output. As steam pressure decreased, the fires went out, and it was the dribbles of oil that caused the vapour. At the front of the boiler room was an upright boiler, which would normally be used in port when the three main boilers were shut down. However, for a number of reasons we were unable to raise steam, as some gear on this donkey boiler was missing.

Before towing could commence we had to get the rudder to a central position. One problem when towing on a long tow is yaw. This was the behaviour of a ship being towed, trying to sheer off in a different direction than the tug. Yaw could be caused by wind blowing or sea running at an angle to the direction of the tow. In the case of the *Sheaf Crown*, the large hole in the port side of No.1 hold had jagged metal plates projecting, causing the ship to sheer to port whilst being towed. By adjusting the headgear to the rudder, we were able to correct this problem as and when conditions changed.

This was one reason why it was decided that the boarding party would stay aboard *Sheaf Crown*. We also had hopes that we might be able to raise steam on at least one of the three main boilers. This would increase our speed from around 4 knots to possibly 7 or 8, by having some assistance from the main engines. The stationary propeller of a large ship can offer a fair amount of resistance, so that working the main engine even at a slow speed can assist, not only in propelling the ship, but overcoming the propeller resistance. When I found out that, for a variety of reasons, raising steam would be a difficult undertaking, we looked at the possibility of disconnecting the main shaft between the engine and the thrust box. But again this was more than we could tackle under the circumstances.

Sub. Lt. Haymer R.N.V.R. was on *Prudent* as 2nd mate, even though he was not a T124T officer. He performed the duties of a relief, and was a member of our boarding party on *Sheaf Crown*. Whilst a greaser and I had been in the engine and boiler room, he and a few of the others had found the wherewithal to supply food and hot drinks. A system of watch keeping had been set up on the auxiliary steering gear to correct any tendency of the ship to steer off course. We unlashed the flat-bottomed wooden punt we found on deck, as we had decided at a very early stage that it would be useful if we ever had to escape from the ship in a hurry. The punt was of the type carried by most merchant ships for painting and doing odd jobs around the shipside in port. Sub Lt Haymer had an understanding of guns, so he had familiarized himself with the 12-pounder on the stern of *Sheaf Crown,* and established a small guns crew.

Somewhere on the bridge they found the cargo manifest, which listed the cargo in the holds and on deck. We were interested to find out what cargo was in No.2 hold, to see if it was giving support to the bulkhead between it and No.1 hold. We soon understood why the ship had been abandoned so smartly. Both No.2 and No.3 hold contained thousands of tons of everything that was horrible in the way of explosives – bombs, mines, torpedoes, cordite charges, shells and bullets. On deck were fighter aircraft in cases. The explosion in No.1 hold, which had blown open the hatch on the port side, had blown open four or five of these cases. It was possible to see the aircraft within. Looking down into the hold one could see hundreds of tons of water rushing into and out of the hole left by the explosion. It was this violent movement of seawater that would put undue strain on the bulkhead of No.2 hold. We thought about putting a tarpaulin over the hole, but soon realised that it would be pretty hopeless in this case, with the jagged edges of the ship's side plates protruding outwards around 10 or 12 feet or more. Another little worry that put us off the idea of fitting a tarpaulin was the odd shark we saw cruising around from time to time. I was in fact carrying my revolver, officially to stop looting, but I always had a feeling it could be handy if I finished up in the water. We wore a lifebelt all the time at sea. It was a very neat affair worn around the waist, made of rubber, encased in a cloth cover and fitted with shoulder straps. Normally it was kept deflated. Clipped onto our shoulder we had a small red light operated by battery.

Our journey on the *Sheaf Crown* was quite uneventful. We all found a comfortable place to sleep, and took turns at watch keeping on the steering and towing wires. We periodically checked bilge water in the engine-room and boiler room. As soon as we arrived aboard, I had checked the main shaft tunnel door and closed it by hand gear. At the end of the third day we arrived off East London just before dark. As *Prudent* was short of fuel, she took in her towing gear. One of the large South African railway tugs came out and took us in tow, up and down the coast off East London until daylight. Just before daylight, Sub Lt. Haymer and I were on the bridge of *Sheaf Crown*. There was a heavy early morning sea mist restricting visibility, so we were unable to see the towing tug. We had been advised that two more tugs were due at daylight, when they would tie up either side of *Sheaf Crown*. This extra assistance was needed, as the entrance to East London harbour was narrow and tricky owing to cross currents at the harbour entrance. Just after daylight the other tugs arrived and tied up alongside just aft of mid-ships. They also brought out a pilot who joined us on the bridge. Whilst talking to him we suddenly noticed a small pointed

16 – Saving The Sheaf Crown And An Incident Of Looting

object travelling at about 8 knots and easily visible in the flat calm sea. The mist was still around and visibility was limited to about 500 or 600 yards. Our first reaction was to shout, "periscope"! Although we could not see the coast, the pilot said we were approximately 4 miles out. Our bows were facing northeast and the "periscope" appeared from our port quarter, made its way across at an angle, and then disappeared into the mist ahead of us. We eventually discovered it was a marker buoy being towed by a fishing boat, which had turned to port and the buoy had swung round in a large circle. The trawler in question was hidden from us by the mist.

By this time we were moving slowly towards East London and the sun was clearing the mist. Whilst talking on the bridge I happened to glance aft, and much to my amazement there were crew members of one of the harbour tugs tossing bundles of looted goods tied up in sheets, over to their tug. By the time I got that far, with revolver in hand, they had seen me coming and disappeared aboard their own ship. I made it clear to two officers on the bridge of the tug that we would report what we had seen, and would carry out our instruction to shoot to stop looting. We suggested they had their ship searched and looted material returned. We locked those cabins with keys in the door and hid the keys. However it was obvious that a good deal of ransacking had taken place.

Very shortly after this episode *Prudent* came out from the harbour and got alongside to pick us up. I had obtained the agreement of our boarding party that we would ask to be searched before leaving *Sheaf Crown*. When *Prudent* came alongside I noticed a senior naval officer on the bridge with our C.O. I hopped aboard *Prudent* leaving our boarding party nearby on the *Sheaf Crown*, in fact quite close to the bridge of *Prudent*. After an introduction to the officer in charge at East London, I quickly explained what had happened regarding the looting and that we all wished to be searched before coming aboard. This was agreed there and then and we all submitted to a search. The naval officer went aboard one of the small naval patrol craft now alongside *Prudent*. We then left for Durban. By this time *Sheaf Crown* was just about to enter harbour.

We were told later that she was eventually repaired and returned to the sea.

Returning to Durban was an event always looked forward to, as most people aboard the ship, including the dog, had somewhere to go. One item of great interest to me was the Sunday evening orchestral concerts in the city hall under the baton of Mr Edward Dunn. Mrs Sexton used to make up a party, which usually included two or three WRENS from the naval base. The WRENS were billeted in a nice hotel on the sea front at Durban.

17 – *The Meliskerk* And The Disappearing Case Of Whisky

OUR NEXT JOB in *Prudent* was an extremely interesting one. We received an urgent call in the early hours of 9th January 1943 to proceed to the Dutch vessel *Meliskerk*, which had run on a reef about 2 miles off Port St Johns, about 120 miles south of Durban. As the call came at about 01.00 hours, a number of people were ashore. It was standing practice when going ashore to leave telephone numbers or addresses where contact could be made. Pat Murray (2nd engineer) and I were with a party at the Stardust Club. It was not very far from our ship, so we were in fact first back aboard. Then there was a delay. Of all people, the C.O. was missing! There was no-one at the address he had given. Fortunately, a sharp eyed sailor reported that he had seen the skipper's car parked behind an all-night mobile coffee stall. I jumped into my Austin and went to this coffee stall, where I found him sound asleep! It was not long before we got underway, as instructions had been given to lift the boom at the harbour entrance. Within about 7 or 8 hours we were at the scene of the grounding. A destroyer was there to take away some gold bullion bound for Ethiopia. The captain, mate and some of the crew were still onboard.

We eventually discovered that the *Meliskerk* was travelling out of convoy, and had been steaming at full speed close to the shore to try and reach Durban before dark on the 8th January 1943. A few feet further to starboard and all would have been well with *Meliskerk*. But she caught the reef with her port side at about 14 knots, causing her to swing to port, finishing up well and truly aground. She faced the coast at right angles to her north easterly course for Durban. When we got aboard we found that Nos.1, 2, 4, and 6 holds were flooded. The engine and boiler rooms were also flooded, and the ship had a list of 15° to starboard. We got our portable pump aboard, having first to take it to pieces. This was because the port deck of *Meliskerk* was too high for our derrick crane, and there was no steam for the winch on the casualty. *Prudent* was unable to approach the starboard side of *Meliskerk* because of the swell and the reef. The first night there was fairly rough, making the job of getting from one ship to the other something of a problem, especially when manhandling our portable diesel driven salvage pump. We set up the diesel pump by No.6 hatch, as requested by the mate, and eventually got it working. But it was soon obvious that the water was entering the hold much quicker than we could pump it out. We had the same result with the engine room.

Eventually it was decided it would not be possible to salvage the *Meliskerk,* and that all effort available would be concentrated on recovering the cargo. The remainder of the crew from the *Meliskerk* were taken aboard, and we returned to Durban for additional equipment, such as 2 ½ inch flexible copper steam piping and large quantities of electric rubber cable. On return to *Meliskerk*, we were able to lie alongside as the weather had improved. From *Prudent* we connected the steam hose to the deck winch steam line on *Meliskerk*, in order to use her winches. An electric cable enabled *Prudent* to supply light into No.4 and 5 holds. There was quite a considerable deck cargo of aircraft in cases, and army lorries. All this was loaded onto coasters sent from Durban. As *Prudent* was alongside the port midships section of *Meliskerk,* the coasters, two at a time, were able to lie ahead and astern of *Prudent*. Once again this ship was carrying war supplies to North Africa, and included in the cargo were many hundreds of tons of munitions. Owing to the nature of the cargo it was decided not to use shore labour, and so the crew of *Prudent* had to work as stevedores. The *Meliskerk* derricks were duly rigged to lift cargo first from the deck, and then from two holds.

In the meantime a request had been received to remove the defensive guns mounted on *Meliskerk*. The machine guns were quite easily removed. Problems arose when we came to tackle the 6-inch gun aft. The 2nd engineer and I studied this thing carefully, and established how to remove the barrel. When we thought the barrel was free we elevated the gun so that it would slide out of its mounting. No such luck! We stood discussing what to do next when I lightly tapped the mounting with a hammer, and out shot about two tons of gun barrel onto the deck, missing various feet by inches. The funniest thing was one fireman who was dumping shells over the side from around the gun platform. When the breach end of the gun barrel struck the wood decking on the gun platform, the fireman was just passing with a shell resting in both arms pressed against his chest. He knew he must not drop it, so he did an amazing jump into the air high enough to clear the gun barrel. Although it could have been serious, it was very funny at the time.

In our early days on *Meliskerk* the mate had shown us where the 'bond' was – the store of spirits, wine, etc. It was mainly 'Bols' gin, but there were also three cases of scotch whisky – a commodity hard to come by at that time. Murray and I hid a case of this whisky up on the boat deck of *Meliskerk*, and thereby hangs a story. It was decided that at a later stage we would launch the two motor lifeboats carried by *Meliskerk* and salvage them. Before doing so, we had to familiarise ourselves with the engines, their fuel type and systems, controls and starting arrangements. Whilst doing this we had to remove a wooden panel from the forward section of one of the motorboats to get at a fuel tank right up in the bows. We decided this would be a good place to hide our case of 12 bottles of whisky. This we did and screwed back the wooden panel. These boats were later launched and tied to the stern of *Prudent*. One evening Murray and I were in Tommy Reed's room making the best of some 'Bols' gin – a drink we never really took to. We let Reed into the whisky secret and decided, as it was dark, to recover the case from the motorboat. Having armed ourselves with a couple of torches, screwdrivers and a length of rope, we proceeded to the after deck. The night was wet, windy and dark and the two boats astern were riding four or five foot waves. We pulled the motorboat we required close up to our rubbing band on the starboard side of *Prudent*, and at the right moment I jumped in. Conditions were very trying as the boat was half full of water which was sloshing about to the extent that I got really soaked and very cold. The others let the motorboat drop back clear of *Prudent* so that it would not get caught under the rubbing band during the rise and fall of the waves. After much effort I was able to get the waterlogged case out. Using a lifting line it was hauled onboard our ship. After replacing the boards in the motorboat, the others pulled the boat forward, and at the right moment I jumped onto the rubbing band and back aboard *Prudent*. By this time the seawater had drained from our case of whisky. It was duly transported to the 3rd engineers' room, where we intended to share the contents. We opened the case and received the shock of our lives – it contained only tins of condensed milk! We never found out who had made the switch and, although the air was somewhat blue at the time, we had many a laugh about it afterwards.

Work went on practically day and night until 26th January 1943. During that day the weather deteriorated so much that it was inadvisable for *Prudent* to remain alongside, as the flexible steam piping to *Meliskerk* was constantly being damaged. As soon as the last coaster left, we went out to anchor. During this lull in proceedings, I suggested to the C.O. that we could do with more water, fuel, flexible steam piping, electric cable and other odd items. A signal was sent off to Durban outlining our requirements and permission was received to proceed there.

We arrived in Durban the next morning and found, as was usual, that our stores were ready for us. Once these were loaded we went for a top up of fuel oil, and then alongside Maydon Wharf for some minor repairs. At the crack of dawn the next day we set off for the *Meliskerk*. We had just passed the halfway mark, when a signal was received to return to Durban. Upon arrival there we were advised that the *Meliskerk* had exploded that morning, and that bits of the ship had been picked up as far as 25 miles inland. From descriptions we heard later, this really was a major explosion. Once again fate took a kindly hand as far as we were concerned. From that day to this I have carried the dice I picked up in the games room on the *Meliskerk*.

A few days later we left Durban to search an area off Port Elizabeth for a torpedoed tanker. On our way we went inshore to see what was left of the *Meliskerk*. All that was visible was the sternpost sticking out of the water at the same angle as the original starboard list of 15 degrees.

Later on that day we were almost at the search area for the tanker, when we were advised by radio that it had sunk and that the crew were in three lifeboats attempting to make for the coast. They were given as around 60 or 70 miles off the coast. Heavy seas and bad visibility were curtailing the activities of the South African Air Force, who had Judson aircraft assisting in the search. In the early stages a destroyer was also searching, but was called away to other duties. We were on this job for about 2½ days, when a signal was received to proceed to East London. Upon arrival there we found that those of us in the boarding party to the *Sheaf Crown* were required to attend a court hearing, concerning the looting which had taken place aboard that ship. Apparently the crew of *Sheaf Crown* had been picked up by an escort and landed in Durban. From there they had returned to their ship to find that the accommodation had been well and truly looted. We were kept hanging about in a cold and draughty corridor of that court building for the best part of two days, whilst we could have been well and usefully employed looking for the tanker survivors. As it was, only one of those three lifeboats made the coast under the command of the mate. The other two were never heard of again. When we were eventually called into court, I became very annoyed by the tone of the questions being asked, in view of the fact that it was us who had reported looting to the local naval commander before we left the *Sheaf Crown*, and we had volunteered to be searched. After leaving East London we heard nothing more of this enquiry. We returned to Durban for boiler cleaning and some leave.

Leave in Durban offered a wide choice, thanks to the hospitality of the South African people. It was possible to obtain details of events and places to visit from the Naval H.Q. who would also make arrangements and issue travel vouchers. There were also service centres where leave could be spent – Johannesburg being the most popular. When there was work going on in the engine and boiler rooms, I liked to stay locally so that I could keep an eye on how work was progressing. Staying with my friends for two or three days was as near to home life as I could get. We enjoyed visits to such places as the Valley of a Thousand Hills, Isapingo Beach, and many others where bathing and picnicking were the order of the day. All too soon boiler cleaning and the various repairs were completed, and we were back 'on station' again. Usually we were on four hours notice, which would from time to time be reduced to two hours, and then to immediate stand by. This indicated that a German U-boat was coming up or down the coast. We discovered later that there was also occasionally an Italian or Japanese submarine. A lot of the troop convoys called in at Durban, bound for Suez or the Indian ports. When these convoys were leaving Durban, the 'Lady in White' would appear in the main dock area, with her hand megaphone and sing such patriotic songs as 'Land of Hope and Glory' as a troop ship, aircraft carrier or other major vessel pulled away from the quayside. I was privileged to see and hear her a number of times. In fact I made a point of doing so, if we were in port when these large ships were leaving. To me it was an extremely moving sight to see this solitary figure against the background of a huge ship, in battle-grey or camouflage, with its decks lined with service personnel silently listening and then cheering at the end of a song. I am quite sure there are many thousands of people who passed through Durban in the war years who will remember the 'Lady in White'.

When not away on a job, we were often required to perform target towing, which was not a very popular pastime. I remember someone from our wardroom met two flight lieutenants on leave from North Africa and invited them aboard for a mid morning drink. It happened that we were target towing the next day and they expressed a desire to come with us. This was arranged, and they arrived aboard at 06.00 hours, shortly before we picked up the target from its moorings. The target was towed alongside the rescue tug until we got clear of the harbour entrance, and then the deep sea towing gear was connected up, with a towing length of around

250 fathoms. In fact the general feeling was that the longer the tow the better. On this occasion the weather was fairly rough, but we were still able to get along at about 10 knots. Our two R.A.F. guests became very sick men, and I can still see them stretched out on the foredeck, not caring much if a practice shell or two did actually hit us.

18 – Madagascar

WHILST WAITING FOR a 'proper' job, we did some more target towing, had a couple of nights ashore, and had a day out at White Sands. Our first real job was to pick up a large French destroyer, which was being towed by a British warship. The weather was reasonable, so it was an easy job towing this destroyer for repair in Madagascar.

We brought her to the large dry dock at Diego Suarez at the northern tip of Madagascar. The official language was French and it had a very racially mixed population of around 27,000. It was an important naval port in the days of French colonisation, and the solidly built dockyard area bore witness to the days when no expense was spared. The soil round about the town and country outside was red in colour. One evening ashore we met two or three army officers who had arrived that day from some remote hill station. After some drinks in a café-bar, they invited us back to the old French barracks where they were spending their few days leave. Most of us climbed into the back of their medium sized army truck, but 2nd engineer Pat Murray elected to sit on the top edge of the tailboard, facing forward. We, the 2nd mate 'Dusty' Miller, the senior wireless operator Duncan Reid and myself, were sitting on seats fixed along the sides of the lorry beneath a canvas cover. The driving was somewhat hectic over a more or less unmade road, which contained some very large puddles. We hit a very deep indent faster than was advisable and Pat Murray disappeared over the back of the lorry! With much hammering and banging on the back of the cab we eventually got the driver to stop. This took a little time because three or four of his pals had been singing and beating time on the cab. After turning round we eventually came across Pat, fortunately unhurt, jumping up and down on his hat in the middle of a puddle big enough to qualify as a pond. Falling flat on to his back into all that water must have saved him from injury. Pat was tall and rather thin, and always immaculately dressed when he went ashore. This particular evening we had on our 'No.10s' –

that is, white uniform cap cover, white long sleeved jacket buttoned up to the neck with shoulder epaulettes showing rank, long white trousers, white socks and white shoes. Bearing all this in mind, Pat was soaked in red mud and water, and looked as though he was bleeding to death from just about everywhere that could bleed. However, the Irish jig he was dancing on his hat and the language being used soon convinced us he was very much alive and unhurt. When we got to the large three or four storied barracks, the army boys were very good. They fixed Pat up with shirt, shorts and shoes, and arranged for his whites to be rinsed out. Our little party went according to plan until the early hours, when our hosts kindly got us back to the ship, and another little bit of irresponsible history was mentally catalogued.

Another point of interest was a British tanker in the dry dock. It had been torpedoed by a Japanese two-man submarine in Diego Suarez whilst it had been supplying fuel oil to the battleship *H.M.S. Ramelles*. The first torpedo hit the *Ramelles*, and the second struck the tanker in the engine-room, killing most of the engine room staff. The tanker had sunk by the stern, and had been salvaged and taken to the dry dock, where we were able to go aboard and take a look at the engine room. The engine was a Sulzer 6 cylinder diesel about 25 feet high by about the same length. The force of the explosion had split the engine in two, so that the rear 3 cylinders and crankcase were laid over in the port aft side, and the other 3 cylinders were laid over in the port forward side of the engine room. This tanker was later towed to Addu Atoll (between Diego Suarez and Colombo) and used as a fuel oil hulk. The *Ramelles* made its way to Simonstown under its own power for repairs. We returned to Durban shortly after this.

19 – Salvaging *U-852*

ONE PEACEFUL DAY, *Prudent* was tied to a buoy in the naval base in Kilindini. Alongside us was one of the 'Epping Forest' naval targets. As the top deck of the hull was only a foot or so above the water, we were using it for bathing sessions in the afternoon. Mombasa is only about 290 miles south of the equator, so the days are very hot indeed. When in port under tropical conditions, the day shift would work from 06.00 hours until 12.00 hours. A reduced crew maintained the normal 4-hour watches. This ensured that the rescue tug would be ready for sea as soon as the rest of the crew had returned to the ship. If we were placed on 4 hours notice or less there would be no shore leave, and those people already ashore would be instructed to return by the naval base. In many ports where the ship's siren could be heard a recall signal of four blasts usually got everyone back. In any case there was a shore leave book in the wardroom for officers, and one at the gangway for other ranks and ratings, giving details of where they were likely to be. In the tropics we used to have a light lunch, and our main meal of the day in the early evening.

Such was the background on the early afternoon of 6th May 1944, when most people were just sunbathing. A signal came aboard requesting the C.O. and chief engineer to report immediately to the office of the flag officer. Upon arrival we were asked for our identity cards, and then directed to a small conference of much gold braid. After introductions and brief preliminaries, we were all handed memorandum number EA 01, headed 'Instructions for search of German submarine ashore off Benda Beila'.

The commanding officer of *H.M.S. Raider* also handed us a 'Report on U boat (*U-852*)' and an Appendix to No EA 01 – CAFO 1477 'Scuttling charges in German U-boats'. (See appendices 4 and 5.) Basically, the discussion centred on how we could get *U-852* sufficiently buoyant to beach her, or at least remove certain equipment from the flooded main hull. The C.O. of *H.M.S. Fishguard* was present at the meeting. He was to be in charge of the operation, and was to provide the protective escort. The memo EA 01 stated, "The possibility of attack by enemy submarine must be borne in mind, and all precautions taken". Commander Fox-Pitt R.N. was detailed to co-ordinate all work on board *U-852*. He proved himself to be an excellent choice for the job. Commander Fox-Pitt and two naval divers with all their gear were embarked aboard *Fishguard*. *Prudent* took aboard an air compressor, quite a lot of flexible 1 inch air hose with various fittings, taps and dies, steel angle iron and flat plate, nuts, bolts and so on.

Benda Beila is on the northern tip of Somalia, about 1350 miles north of Mombasa, at 10ºN and 51ºE. The weather was very calm and warm, and so it only took us about 3 days to get there. We made such good progress that we were ordered to slow down in order to arrive in early morning daylight. *U-852* was quickly located about 200 yards off a very rocky coast, with a sandy beach just to the north-east of its stern. *Prudent* anchored about 300 yards to the south-east, in order to keep clear of unexploded depth charges known to have been dropped on a track to the south of the U-boat. The damage caused to *U-852* by depth charges caused her to surface. She was unable to dive again, and was very vulnerable to R.A.F. aircraft working from Aden. Their harassment forced the U-boat commander to abandon ship, after measures had been taken to scuttle her. Charges were placed in the forward and after ends of the U-boat, and the crew made for the shore in rubber inflatable life rafts. The last job on the U-boat was to……

Note from the Editor
The narrative ends here abruptly. Stanley Butler's life ended just as abruptly when he died suddenly of a heart attack in June 1979 aged just 66 years old.

To finish the story I did some research on *U-852* and discovered a very complex and fascinating story. The best article I found on this subject was by Dwight R Messimer, called 'Siegerjustiz and the *Peleus* Affair'. I have condensed this article and combined it with an Admiralty report on the salvage.

20 – *U-852* And The *Peleus* Affair

HEINZ-WILHELM ECK WAS born in Hamburg on 27 March 1916. He joined the German Merchant Navy in 1934 and served mostly on mine sweepers. In June 1942 Eck volunteered for service in U-boats. After four months learning the basics, he joined *U-124* as Captain-In-Training. On 1 June 1943 he assumed command of the newly constructed *U-852*.

By 18 January 1944, sea trials had been completed and they were ready to set out on their first tour of duty. They were tasked with leaving Kiel and sailing to Penang in Malaysia. This was *U-852's* first and last mission. In the weeks leading up to their departure, Captain Eck sought the advice of his colleagues. Captain Adalbert Schnee was ranked as one of Germany's most successful U-boat commanders. He warned Eck about the strong air cover in the Atlantic Narrows, especially between Freetown and Ascension Island. Schnee pointed out that wreckage from a torpedoed ship would be seen by enemy forces, alerting them to the presence of a U-boat. Four U-boats had already been lost in the South Atlantic near Ascension Island. Eck must have taken this advice to heart, as it was to lead to his downfall.

Sailing down the coast of West Africa, it took them two months to reach the equator. On 13 March, a lookout spotted a freighter ahead off the starboard bow. They were 500 miles north of Ascension Island and 700 miles south of Freetown. The ship was the Greek registered *SS Peleus*, which was 6,659 tons. It was dark before *U-852* was in a position to attack. At 19.40 she fired two torpedoes, which both hit the *Peleus*. Captain Eck wrote in his log, "...the detonation was very impressive". Survivors reported that *Peleus* sank so quickly that most of the crew of 35 didn't have time to put on a life vest. The rafts stored on deck were amongst the debris left on the surface after the ship sank.

As *U-852* approached the debris field they heard whistles and shouting. They also saw lights from some of the rafts. U-boat captains were instructed that, whenever possible, they should question survivors about the cargo and the destination of their ship. To conduct the questioning of survivors, Eck ordered two English speakers on deck. They were the Chief Engineer Hans Lenz and the Second Watch Officer August Hoffman.

The U-boat approached a life raft containing *Peleus's* Third Officer Agis Kephalas, greaser Stavros Sagians and a Russian seaman called Pierre Neuman. Kephalas was brought onboard the U-boat to be questioned on the deck. He told them that the ship was in ballast, and was heading from Freetown to the River Plate in South America. This Greek officer was returned to his life raft after questioning and told that the surviving crew would be picked up the following day by the British.

As *U-852* proceeded on her way, Lenz gave his report to Eck. At that point there were five officers on the bridge. They were Captain Eck, First Officer Colditz, Second Officer Hoffmann, Chief Engineer Lenz and Doctor Weispfennig. Eck told Colditz and Lenz of his concern about the amount of wreckage. He was sure that this debris would be spotted in the morning by an enemy air patrol. By running on the surface at high speed until dawn, the submarine could travel nearly 200 miles. However, Eck was worried that this was not far enough away to avoid detection, and so he took the fateful decision to return to the wreckage and destroy all traces of the *Peleus*.

Colditz and Lenz both expressed their opposition to this decision. The captain listened to their objections but his mind was not changed. Eck justified his decision as an "operational necessity", as it was his duty to protect his boat from discovery and destruction. Lenz left the bridge at this time to write his report and carry out his duties below deck. Captain Eck ordered two machine guns to be brought up to the bridge. They were mounted on railings on the port and starboard sides, and by 8 pm they were ready to open fire. The rafts could barely be seen, as it was a dark moonless night. Dr. Weispfennig was standing next to the starboard gun when Eck ordered him to fire on the wreckage. He aimed at a raft approximately 200 yards away and fired several short bursts. The gun soon jammed and Hoffmann stepped forward to clear the jam. Hoffmann continued firing, but with no apparent effect. Despite receiving many rounds of ammunition, the raft showed no signs of sinking. Eck had thought that the rafts were mounted on hollow floats that would take in water when they were punctured. The rafts were in fact made of a solid buoyant material. Hours past as the U-boat moved slowly through the wreckage, firing when they could see a raft. After some time, Hoffmann suggested that they should use the 37mm gun, which had explosive shells. Using the 105mm deck gun was also considered. Eck dismissed both these ideas as he thought the targets were too close. However Captain Eck did order hand-grenades to be brought on deck. The only person known to have thrown grenades was Hoffmann. It is not known how many were used.

Chief engineer Lenz was not on the bridge during the first four hours when the lifeboats were fired on. He returned after midnight, just as Schwender was clearing a jam on the port side machine gun. Lenz took control of the gun and opened fire on a raft. During his trial it could not be established why he had taken control of the gun, as he had not been ordered to do so by the captain.

Antonios Liossis had been the chief officer onboard the *Peleus*. As he sat on one of the rafts, he was alarmed when he realised that the U-boat had returned to the area. At the sound of gun fire, he dived onto the floor of the raft. He heard Demitrios Rostantinidis cry out as he died in a hail of bullets. Sometime later, Liossis was wounded in the shoulder by shrapnel from a grenade thrown from *U-852*. In another raft, Agis Kephalas was sheltering with two seamen. As the U-boat passed them, the two seamen were killed, and Kephalas was injured in the arm. Kephalas slipped from the raft, and was able to swim to the raft containing Liossis. The rafts drifted for 35 days before a ship picked them up. There were only 3 survivors. Kephalas was not one of them.

Captain Eck spent five hours trying to destroy the wreckage, but only succeeded in killing and injuring some of the survivors. At 1 am he ordered *U-852* to sail out of the area at top speed.

News of what had been happening had spread through the crew and morale was very low. The general feeling was that it was unjust to kill survivors. Eck felt it necessary to address the crew on the loudspeaker system to explain his actions. He told them that it was "with a heavy heart" that he had ordered the destruction of the rafts. He did not want the survivors to die, but he needed to sink the rafts, so that they were not discovered by enemy search planes. Eck said that the crew should not have too much sympathy for the crew of the *Peleus,* but to think of their own wives and children at home, who were being killed by enemy air raids. This pep talk did nothing to change the distaste the crew felt for what had happened.

Even though they delayed their departure by five hours, *U-852* was able to leave the area undetected. They sailed south for the next two weeks, without incident. However, their presence in the area had been noted. On 15 March, Eck sent a radio message to U-boat headquarters regarding the sinking of the *Peleus*. This transmission was picked up by radio detection finders and information was passed on to the British naval authorities in Capetown.

On 1 April, Eck torpedoed and sank the freighter *SS Dahomian*, just south-west of Cape Point. The British reacted to this swiftly, dispatching an anti-submarine warfare group to hunt down the U-boat. They carried out an intensive search for three days, but did not make contact. On 4 April Eck sent a long radio message to U-boat headquarters. Radio detection posts gave the British a position for the submarine as 150 miles east-south-east of Point Agulhas. Eck must have been skilled at avoiding detection, because he stayed in the Capetown area for a further 2 weeks undetected. As they were not able to sink any ships during this time, Eck decided to sail north towards Penang.

Around this time, the survivors from the *SS Peleus* were rescued by the Portuguese steamer *SS Alexandre Silva*. Only three men were still alive. They were chief officer Antonios Liossis, greaser Rocco Said and seaman Dimitrios Argiros. One week later they docked at Lobito, Angola. Reports were filed and passed on to the British Admiralty. Later, the survivors were interviewed by British intelligence officers.

U-852 sailed up the east coast of Africa. These were very dangerous waters for them, as a hunter-killer group had been assigned to the area. This comprised of nine frigates and sloops, with the escort carriers *HMS Begum* and *HMS Shah*. The Indian Ocean was also patrolled by aircraft flying from Addu Atoll and Diego Garcia.

By 30 April, *U-852* had sailed up the east coast as far as the Horn of Africa. This was the southernmost tip of the Gulf of Aden. By remaining submerged during daylight hours, the U-boat had avoided contact with her pursuers. However, British intelligence had placed her in the area. RAF Wellington bombers were sent out each day to search for them off the coast of Somaliland (now called Somalia).

Just before dawn on 2 May, a group of Wellington bombers spotted *U-852* cruising on the surface. Lieutenant Hoffmann and the other look-outs were taken completely by surprise when the planes dived at them from out of the sun. The U-boat was strafed and bombed. Six depth charges were dropped and at least one of them found its target. They were able to submerge before the planes could make a second run, but the damage had already been done. In addition to water flooding in, deadly chlorine gas from damaged batteries was filling the submarine. They were forced to surface after 15 minutes. As soon as they surfaced, the gun crews rushed on deck to man the guns. They were strafed repeatedly by the Wellingtons, and Oberleutnant Colditz and crewman Josef Hafer were killed on the bridge.

Captain Eck knew that the U-boat was finished. They were unable to submerge, and the stern was down from flooding. He decided that the best way to save the crew was to beach the boat on the coast of Somaliland. It was afternoon before they reached the coast. For most of the day, the gun crews had been fighting off attacks by enemy planes. They beached the submarine at Ras Hafun, and most of the crew were able to escape to the beach. Eck had given orders to abandon ship and for charges to be set to destroy her. The demolition did not go according to plan. One crew member was killed and the charges only partially destroyed the submarine. The standing orders to destroy the War Diary were not carried out. It contained the incriminating details of the attack on the *Peleus*, and was used in the war crimes trial against Eck and other members of his crew.

Many of the crew jumped straight into the sea and swam towards the beach. A few stayed behind to help the wounded into rubber rafts. Even though the crew were obviously abandoning ship, they were machine gunned by the attacking Wellingtons. (This is an interesting point to note, as crew members from the submarine were later charged with attacking survivors from the *Peleus*). Second Officer Hoffmann was shot in the leg as he assisted a badly wounded man into a raft. The crew spent the night on the beach.

The next day they were taken prisoner by a British Navy landing party, assisted by the Somaliland Camel Corps. Thirty-four members of the crew were transported to Aden, where they were questioned by Lieutenant Burnett RNVR. He was the head of the Naval Section, Combined Special Detachment Intelligence Collection (CSDIC). Burnett interrogated them for two weeks, and then arranged for their transfer to Cairo. He gave orders that twelve of the crew should be separated from the rest. Intelligence officer J. T. Rugh USNR questioned the remaining group of 22 for another two weeks. Certain crew members told stories about survivors from the *Peleus* being shot at in the water and in rafts.

Burnett visited the wreck of *U-852* and obtained the war-diary. On his return to Cairo, he compared notes with Rugh. They knew that it was *U-852* that sank the *Peleus*, and had statements from survivors that said that they were shot at in their life rafts. Burnett and Rugh looked for more evidence that could be used in a war crimes trial. They confronted Chief Engineer Hans Lenz with their findings, and he confirmed them. He signed an affidavit detailing his memories of the events. Crew members Johann Coirniak and Wilhelm Schmidtz were confronted next. They also signed affidavits detailing events. The three survivors from the *Peleus* were flown to Capetown to give evidence. Their sworn affidavits were dated 7 June 1944.

Shortly after this, Heinz Eck, August Hoffmann, Walter Weispfennig, Hans Lenz and Walter Schwender were flown to England. They spent the next 16 months in prison awaiting trial.

The information used in this chapter was taken from an article by Dwight R Messimer, called 'Siegerjustiz And The Peleus Affair'.

21 – The Salvage Operation

IN 2006 I wrote to the Royal Navy to see if they still had any documents on the salvage of *U-852*. They were very helpful, and directed me to The National Archives at Kew, Surrey. I was able to obtain the report by the senior officer directing the salvage, Commander Thomas Fox-Pitt. What follows is a condensed account of his report.

Cmd. Fox-Pitt arrived off the coast of Bender Beila on 14 May and took charge of the salvage operation. *HMS Fishguard* and *HMRT Prudent* had arrived some days earlier and had commenced operations. As the depth of the water around *U-852* was only about 15 feet, the recovery ships had been stationed at least 400 feet away from it. It was known that there were 6 depth charges in the vicinity, and so ships were warned to anchor clear of the submarine. The only vessel with a sufficiently shallow draught to be moored next to the U-boat was a lighter, which had been brought by *HMS Fishguard*. *Prudent* had a draught of 18 feet, and so was moored 600 feet from the shore. Despite this, her crew were able to run an air-line over to the salvage and diving pumps situated on the lighter. This air-line powered the pneumatic drills used on the submarine. *Prudent*'s motor boat was the only power boat available for the operation.

The stern and bow sections of *U-582* had been badly damaged by explosions. At first it was thought that bulkhead doors, forward and aft of the main compartment, could be sealed watertight. This would allow the main compartment to be pumped dry, buoyancy would be increased, and the U-boat could possibly be taken under tow. Unfortunately, the door at the aft end had been distorted by an explosion and could not be sealed.

The weather was good when the salvage operation started, but it grew steadily worse over the following days, to a point where it was difficult to get the salvage crews off the stricken vessel. The men started work at first light, which was 06.15. Corned beef along with biscuits and tea were sent over to them during the morning.

Weather permitting, the men would work until 15.00. Usually, as day progressed, the wind would steadily increase to its full force. The salvage ships would be moved down wind to pick up the small boats transferring the crew. In the following extract from his report, Cmd. Fox-Pitt describes the appalling conditions that the men had to endure:

"Those men worked inside the submarine for hours on end in the days when her stability was uncertain. As the wind and sea increased and the swell began to run, she lurched and crashed as the big seas broke on her. Down below it was dark except for the isolated flow of torches; no light was reflected from the dull slime that covered the paint work. There was the stink of fuel and rotting food from blown tins; there was a rush and swirl of oil and water over the floor boards, and sudden cascades down the hatch or periscope glands as seas broke on the conning tower.

It was a horrible place to work in for a short time with the excuse of other work to take one out into the sun again but these men with many others worked down there for hours. There was the constant unspoken threat that every lurch would list her over beyond the point of balance and they would be trapped with the conning tower hatch under the water. There was no one whose duty took him down who held back.

I must also mention those individuals who did outstanding work in saving the torpedoes and telescopes, in working the boats and securing the wires and moorings.

The Commanding Officer and Boatswain's Party of the SENNEN, who hoisted out the after periscope.

The first Lieutenant and Torpedo Party of the OSIRIS, who saved two torpedoes.

Lieutenant Eyre who jacked up a torpedo container so that the torpedo could be withdrawn. Also for handling the boats at the edge of the surf in a very seamanlike manner.

Petty Officer Kay and a party from the SENNEN, who re-moored the lighter in a heavy sea.

Lieutenant Crump, the Chief Boatswains Mate, and the Boatswain's Party of HMS FISHGUARD, who lifted the gun and secured it on the lighter.

The Coxswain and the crew of HMRT PRUDENT's motor boat, who handled their boat in a most seamanlike way.

Lieutenant (E) Wilson, RN, HMS OSIRIS. He was responsible for the pumping, and spent more time below than anyone else. He set a good example when unpleasant and dangerous work had to be done. His knowledge of submarine construction was invaluable.

Lieutenant Clayton, RNVR Port Radar Officer, Kilindini. The successful recovery of the radar unit was due to his energy. He worked in conditions of horrible discomfort and apparent danger with great cheerfulness and concentration.

Stoker Petty Officer W. Morgan, D/KX 88644, HMS OSIRIS. He was a pioneer of every attempt to enter the submarine and was always there when difficulties arose and always did the right thing.

Diver French (Rating: Plumber) C/MX 118903, Kilindini Dockyard. French was always willing to take risks. Although the youngest of the divers he did far more than any of them.

Stoker R Daley, D/SKX 968, HMS OSIRIS. He worked harder than any other man and spent long hours below in the endless work of clearing sections and shifting pump hoses.

Leading Stoker J Birkshire, P/DX 138412, HMS OSIRIS. He undertook the most difficult and unpleasant work and was cheerful and busy under the most beastly conditions.

E.R.A. (D) F Scotney (C/MX 504891 of Kilindini Dockyard). He was given a number of difficult jobs to do in the submarine and did them with great perseverance and skill."

Cmd. Fox-Pitt also commented that, "...the underwater burning gear supplied...was most unsatisfactory and none of the divers had any experience of working with it." This may be why they were unable to remove the obstacles blocking their way into the forward compartments.

The most valuable items recovered from the submarine included confidential books of call signs, charts showing minefields and U-boat routes, *U-852's* log, diagrams of pipe lines and electrical circuits, radar units, the periscope, two torpedoes, electrical fittings, echo sounding units, specimens of ammunition, and the AA guns and their mountings.

On 5 June, the salvage crew attempted to remove the radar units, which held the connections and wiring to the supply. They were going to cut them up and pass the pieces through the hatch in the conning tower. It was thought that they were made of steel and attempts were made to cut them with a burning torch. It was soon discovered that they were made of an aluminium alloy and produced such fumes that the burner could not cut the metal. The report suggested that hack saws could be used to cut up the units. This was planned for the next day. Unfortunately, the lighter sank that night. The barrel of the 4.1 inch gun had been lashed to the lighter. This gave her a list, and may have caused her to sink. The pumps on board her were unusable and so the salvage operation was brought to an end.

The information in this chapter came from file ADM 1/29753, The National Archives.

22 – Honoured By The King

FOR THEIR VALIANT work on the salvage of *U-852*, eleven men were recommended for honours. Stanley Butler was awarded a 'mention in dispatches'. He was presented with a bronze oak-leaf emblem to signify the award. This was to be worn on the ribbon of the War Medal 1939-45. Commander Fox-Pitt wrote the following recommendation for Stanley Butler:

"During the operation of salvaging gear from U-852, Sub-Lieutenant Butler was untiring in keeping pumps and motor boat running. On 20th of May, when the submarine had taken further list and was rolling in an alarming manner, he set a good example by remaining below in her for most of the day."

Medals awarded to Stanley Butler for service 1939 – 1945.

23 – The Trial

IN OCTOBER 1945, Captain Eck and four of his crew were transferred from their prison in England to Alton prison in Hamburg. By that time the war had ended, and Germany was occupied by allied forces.

The men were formally charged with war crimes on 6 October. The trial was due to start only four days later, giving the defence team just three days to prepare their case. It was unlikely that any documents they ordered would arrive before the trial. None of the German lawyers were familiar with British court procedures, and they wanted time to study international law. For these reasons an adjournment was requested. Presiding over the trial was Judge Advocate Major A. Melford Stevenson KC. He refused the request for an adjournment, and ordered that the trial should proceed without delay.

The warrant which empowered the British military court in Germany was issued in June 1945. They could try cases '... in violation of the laws and usages of war ...'. The term 'usages of war' meant the rules of war, and was supposed to define acceptable behaviour for the armed forces. However, what was regarded as acceptable behaviour had changed over time. In the 1914-18 war, it was considered a crime to torpedo a merchant ship without warning. By 1939 the 'usages of war' had changed, and merchant ships were attacked without warning. There were examples of British, American and German forces taking actions that would result in the death of survivors, justified because these actions were considered to be an 'operational necessity'.

Captain Eck and four others were charged with '...being concerned in the killing of members of the crew...by firing and throwing grenades at them.' The fact that Eck ordered his crew to fire at the wreckage was not in dispute. What the defence team needed to do was show that Eck had no specific intent to kill the survivors. It was his duty to protect his boat and crew, and so it was an 'operational necessity' to destroy the large pieces of wreckage.

The likelihood that survivors would be killed as a result of his actions had become acceptable under the 'usages of war'.

The case for the prosecution was presented in less than three hours. The defence team objected to the affidavits from the *Peleus* survivors being read out to the court, as they were unable to cross-examine the witnesses from the Greek ship. Their objections were overruled, and these statements were admitted as evidence. Five crew members from *U-852* were cross-examined. None of these witnesses said that the survivors were fired on deliberately. They said that Captain Eck had ordered them to destroy the rafts, but never gave orders to shoot at survivors.

Captain Eck was on the stand for a day and a half. His personal manner did not help his case, as his answers were short and abrupt. His defence team failed to provide Eck with the opportunity to expand his answers. The prosecution were very skilful in the way they worded their questions, forcing Eck to give answers that showed him in a bad light. The defence team could have countered this by giving Eck prompts that would help him to justify his actions. Hoffmann also did badly during cross examination. The prosecution were able to establish that he had not received a direct order from Eck to fire at the lifeboats, and that he was the only one to throw hand grenades. Even though Dr Weispfennig was actually ordered to fire by the Captain, he did not have to comply. As a medical doctor he was a non-combatant, and specifically prohibited from taking up arms except in self defence. The tribunal found no defence for his actions.

Towards the end of the third day the case from both sides had been heard, and they were called upon to make their closing statements. The chief defence lawyer asked for this to be delayed until the next day, to give him time to prepare. He stated again that the defence team were unfamiliar with British military law and that they had had little sleep over the previous three nights, as they had been preparing their case. Their request was denied.

After the closing speeches, it took the seven members of the tribunal only 58 minutes to reach a verdict. Eck, Hoffman and

Weispfennig were sentenced to death by firing squad. Chief Engineer Lenz received life imprisonment, and enlisted man Wolfgang Schwender was sentenced to 15 years in prison. On 30 November 1945, Captain Eck, First Officer Hoffmann and Dr Weispfennig were executed in the exercise yard of Alton Prison.

Supporters of Eck argued that he had been treated unfairly, and should have been convicted of manslaughter. They drew attention to the much more lenient attitude shown in other cases when survivors were shot at in the water by British and American forces. One example was the case of the German destroyer *Erich Giese*, which was sunk near Narvik on 13 April 1940. German survivors later testified that they were fired on by British destroyers whilst they were in lifeboats.

It was an interesting coincidence that two of the defence lawyers died shortly after the trial. Dr Pabst was said to have committed suicide and Dr Todsen was killed when his car was hit by a British Army truck. Both deaths were investigated by British Military Police, but their report has never been made public. In the years following the trial, the sentences were reviewed. Wolfgang Schwender was freed on 21 December 1951. Hans Lenz was released from prison on 27 August 1952.

This chapter is a brief summary of an article written by Dwight R Messimer called 'Siegerjustiz And The Peleus Affair'.

Epilogue

I'm fortunate to have my father's 'Continuous Service of Discharge', which resembles a passport. According to this he was discharged from *HMRT Prudent* in Simonstown, South Africa, on 29 January 1945.

He married my mother, Patsy Kenny, in Glasgow on 11 April 1945. They had been engaged for three years. They didn't have much time for a honeymoon, as he had to make his way to Harwich the next week to join *HMRT Enticer*. Eight days later he was instructed to join *HMRT Griper* in Falmouth. My father was on *Griper* from 30 April 1945 until 29 March 1946, when he was discharged in Singapore.

Unfortunately, I can only recount one anecdote from that period. This was a story about how he was nearly killed a few weeks before my sister Anne was born, which was in March 1946. At that time *Griper* was in Sumatra in the Dutch East Indies (now called Indonesia). After an entertaining evening ashore, my father and four others were driving back to their ship when they were stopped by the British Military Police. These Redcaps informed them that only four people were allowed to travel in a jeep. The *Griper* crew tried to argue that there was only one jeep, it was late at night, and they all needed to get back to their ship. But this was not allowed, and so it was decided that my father and another person would walk back to the ship.

At that time some of the locals were fighting for independence from the Dutch. Unfortunately, the British and Dutch naval uniforms were similar and difficult to tell apart. As my father and his companion were walking along the street, a man on a rooftop started firing a machine gun at them. As he ran for cover he saw chunks of the road being thrown up near him by the bullets. They both got back to the *Griper* uninjured, but with a lifelong dislike for "jobs-worth Redcaps".

Stanley Butler was discharged from the *Griper* the day after Anne was born, and was demobbed in Harwich on 28 May 1946. He never actually returned to sea, although this was his original intention. I have a copy of a letter he wrote in 1979 describing what happened when he was looking for a merchant ship to join. He wrote: *"… I phoned them to find out what they had in hand, and they told me to 'proceed forthwith' to Hong Kong to join Enticer. My wife and daughter were not well at the time, so I decided at the last minute not to go. Enticer (W166) was lost in a typhoon with all hands on 21 December 1946. I read about it in the newspaper, and it reminded me of the time I spent out there before the war".* In my opinion, he didn't return to sea because after losing his first wife and son in 1941, he didn't want to be away from his new family for long periods of time.

My father got a good job as a technical sales rep for the American oil company Caltex, and so the family moved to Ireland. They lived in Dublin for 12 years, where my brother John and I were born.

The next house he bought was in Sheffield, just five miles from the beautiful Derbyshire Peak District. He worked for The National Coal Board until he retired in 1973. He never lost his passion for engines, and was a founder member of both The National Traction Engine Club and The Sheffield and District Steam Society.

At the time of his death in June 1979, as well as writing this book, he had a lathe and workshop in his garage and was building a miniature steam locomotive from the plans for 'Highland Lassie'. He died peacefully in his chair one morning. He had a mid-morning nap after cutting the grass, and never woke up. What a fabulous way to go – I should be so lucky!

Pete Butler – July 2020.

The wedding of Stanley Butler and Patsy Kenny on 11 April 1945.

Prudent was sold in 1947, was renamed Cautious, and became a dockyard tug. In 1964 she was sold to a Canadian company and renamed Rivtow Lion. She was deliberately sunk on 6 April 2005 to become a recreational dive site, at Nanaimo, British Columbia, Canada.

Appendix One

Ships That Stanley Butler Served In Before Joining The Rescue Tug Service

M.V. Backworth. As 4th Engineer. 15th April 1937 to 10th June 1937. Destination Barbados.

M.V. Lumen. As 4th Engineer. 23rd July 1937 to 19th January 1938. Two voyages to the USA.

S.S. Darcoila. As 4th and 3rd Engineer. 3rd February 1938 to 22nd March 1939;
South Shields, Elba, Port Said, Aden, Calcutta, Yokohama, Kushiro, Muroran, Tokyo, Yokohama, Osaka, Kobe, Moji, Dairen, Yingkow, Chinnampa, Kawasaki, Tokyo, Yokohama, Osaka, Kobe, Moji, Dairen, Inchon, Nagoya, Yokohama, Rashin, Magasaki, Sabang, Port Said, Rotterdam, Kiel, Copenhagen, West Hartlepool.

M.T. British Triumph. As 4th Engineer. 29th July 1939 to 14th November 1939;
Thameshaven, Aberdan, Aden, Capetown, Freetown, Ellesmere Port, Stanlow, Birkenhead.

S.S. Sithonia. As 3rd Engineer. 5th January 1940 to 3rd May 1940; Birkenhead, Barry, Las Palmas, Tenerife, Houston, Newport News, Halifax Nova Scotia, Glasgow. From 4th May 1940 to 20th August 1940; Glasgow, Panama City, Houston, Texas City, Pensacola, Newport News, Halifax, Swansea.

The Fate Of Some Of These Ships

DARCOILA. Douglas & Ramsey, Lithgows, 4084 tons.
370 x 50.6 x 24.9, 424 N.H.P. Triple Expansion Engines. Coal Burner. *Darcoila* left Milford Haven on 20th September 1940 on a voyage in ballast to Philadelphia. She was never seen again. It was thought that she was sunk by a submarine on 28th or 29th September 1940.

BRITISH TRIUMPH. British Tanker Co, built 1936 by Lithgows, 4986 tons.
476.6 x 611.7 x 33.9, 490 N.H.P. B & W Oil Engines.
Outward bound from Hull to Aruba, *British Triumph* struck a mine just off The Wash, and sank on 12th February 1940.

SITHONIA. H.M. Thompson, built 1919 by (Radnorshire) J.L. Thompson & Sons, 6723 tons. 412.5 x 55.5 x 34.4 ; 597 N.H.P. Triple Expansion Engines. Coal Burner.
Whilst on a voyage from Barry to Montevideo, *Sithonia* was torpedoed and sunk by a German submarine on 12th July 1942, about 400 miles west of Tenerife. Six of her crew and one gunner were lost.

Details were taken from *'Dictionary of Disasters at Sea during the Age of Steam'* by Charles Hocking, (2 volumes). Published by Lloyd's Register of Shipping, 71 Fenchurch Street, London.

Appendix Two

Assurance Class Tugs

Both *Restive* and *Prudent* were Assurance class tugs. These tug hulls were built by Cochrane Shipbuilders Ltd of Selby. Machinery was produced by Charles D Holmes & Co Ltd of Hull.

Displacement was 700 tons, length 157 feet overall, beam 33.5 feet, mean draught 10.5 feet. They had a triple expansion reciprocating steam engine of 1,350 Indicated Horse Power, driving a single shaft. This delivered a service speed of 13 knots.

Armament was one 3 inch gun for surface and anti-aircraft protection, two 20 mm anti-aircraft guns, two machine guns, plus some rifles and revolvers.

The usual crew strength was 31 men.

Pennant Number	Name	Date Launched	Date Lost	Cause
W 107	ADEPT	25.08.1941	17.03.1942	Wrecked on Sanda Island.
W 108	ADHERENT	24.09.1941	14.01.1944	Floundered in North Atlantic.
W 50	ALLEGIANCE	22.02.1943		
W 141	ANTIC	24.07.1943		
W 142	ASSIDUOUS	04.06.1943		
W 59	ASSURANCE	23.05.1940	18.10.1941	Wrecked at entrance to Lough Foyle.
W 109	CHARON	21.11.1941		
W 111	DEXTEROUS	03.04.1942		
W 143	EARNER	03.07 1943		
W 11	FRISKY	27.05.1941		
W 112	GRIPER	16.05.1942		

Pennant Number	Name	Date Launched	Date Lost	Cause
W 110	HENGIST	20.12.1941		
W 97	HORSA	29.07.1942	16.03.43	Wrecked on east coast of Iceland.
W 30	JAUNTY	11.06.1941		
W 96	PROSPEROUS	29.06.1942		
W 73	PRUDENT	06.08.1940		
W 39	RESTIVE	04.09.1940		
W 131	SAUCY	26.10.1942		
W 144	SESAME	01.10.1943	11.06.1944	Torpedoed by a German E Boat.
W 87	STORMKING	24.11.1942		
W 18	TENACITY	22.06.1940		

Appendix Three

Letters Received

Stanley Butler placed advertisements in magazines asking for information from ex-HMRTS personnel. Below is a summary of the letters he received.

1. **Haylett, K. R.** from Sidmouth. Was Mate, later Commanding Officer. Joined service May 1943. Was on *Salvonia* in Gibraltar under Lieut. McCabe. From Campbeltown January 1944 to Hull as No.1 of *Envoy* (new). Late 1944 on *Freedom* under Lt. Comm. Tim Bond. In early 1945 was on *Reward* under Lt Bobbie. In Portsmouth and on *Tenacity* as Commanding Officer. Then to *Enigma* in Singapore. At D Day + 1, towed block ships, floating bridges and finally 10000 blocks for Mulberry Harbour. Then to American beach 'Omaha'. In *Reward* at first landing in Channel Islands (St Helena). Then to Cape Town, Durban and Singapore.
2. **Nelson, Jim** from Manchester. Captain of tug on Manchester Ship Canal.
3. **Shannon, E.** from Sheerness. In 1942 on dockyard tugs in Sheerness. 1943 went into R.F.A. until 1953. Served on salvage ships, oilers and store ships. Worked on tugs *Earner, Saucy, Envoy, Cautious* and *Dexterous.* Also on salvage ships *Kinbrace, Kinloss, Lifeline, Lady Southborough, Dapper, Southampton Salvo, Succour* and *Salvictor.*
4. **Spencer, R.J.** from Wakefield. Was 2nd Mate in Admiralty salvage ships *Salvage Duke* and *Salventure*. Ships worked on were *Dorset Coast, Genepesca, Lwow, Jonathon Worth, Bolsta, Valloda, Marianina Rosa M, Ada WT 113*, Schooner *FPV2021*, Italian Minesweeper *Folaga, Thamesfield*, L.C.I. and L.C.F.

5. **Thornley, Terry R.** from London. Was 2nd Mate, 1st Mate, and acting C.O. on *Eminent, Seaman, Danube V, Empire Lawson, Enticer, Griper*. Discussed Captain Sanders, Harwich, Lieut. A.S. Pike R.N.R., Lt Comdr. Harry Anton R.N.R., Sub Lt. McCartney R.N.V.R.
6. **Churchard** from East Germany. Was Stoker 1st Class from 1945 to 1947. Served on *Growler, Assiduous,* and *Samper Peratus*. *Growler* and *Reward* towed floating dock from Durban to Singapore. *Reward* broke down near Seychelles. December 1945 on *Assiduous* in Keppel Docks, waited in dry docking for 21 months. Mentions "*Highland Brigade*" or "*Highland Monarch*" being mined. *Benlomond* was also mined. *S.S. Francis Serves* went aground in USA.
7. **Dodd, I.R.** from Dover. Signalman 1945. 1946 on *Warden*. Floating Dock No. 5 from Alexandria (Egypt) to Bermuda 3 months, assisted by *Reward*. Stand-by tug was *Enchanter*. Father was lost in *Englishman*. Had M.C. from 1st world war. After war was on *Masterman* and *Welshman* as Radio Officer.
8. **Durrant R.O.** from Lowestoft. In May 1945 was training at Campbeltown. Was on *Minora* and *Saucy*. Towed U-boats to Atlantic for scuttling from Stranraer. *Minora* closed January 1946. February 1946 to *Prosperous* in Londonderry. Duty tug Western Approaches. Assistance to *Packisham* loaded with wood pulp, towed through bad weather to Clyde. *Georgetown Victory* well ashore on rocks south of Belfast – could not assist. Towed large concrete blocks from south Scotland to Portland for "sub-base". *Saucy* laid up at Harwich. Demobbed in January 1947 aged 18 years 11 months. Went on to R.F.A. Tugs.
9. **Dymond, D.J.** from Ashtead. Involved in Catering. P.O. Steward on *Caroline Moller, Adherent, Bustler, Empire Ace* and *Mindful*.

10. **Evenden, J.W.** from Hull. (Awarded M.B.E.) Commanding Officer, Lieut. R.N.R. of *Restive, Saucy, Growler*. (Elder brother of Trinity House).
11. **Finley, Campbell.** Radio Officer from September 1942 to September 1946. Campbeltown. U.S.A. Orange, Texas. *Advantage* April 1943 commissioned, then to Bermuda until September 1944. After this returned to U.K. via St Johns towing *Director* to Clyde. *Advantage* to Falmouth. Sailed to Far East December 1944. Mentions R.T.s *Eminent, Cheerly* and *Destiny*, and also *Cambrian Salva*. Refit in Sydney. Hong Kong. Handed over in Philippines to U.S. Navy. *Weasel* to Hong Kong. *Encore* for 2 months. To *H.M.S. Badger* in Harwich. Mentions 2nd Radio Officer Clifford Stokes. Demobbed in *H.M.S. Suffolk* in May 1946.

Appendix Four

Instructions For Search Of German Submarine

The text below is copied from a document found amongst Stanley Butler's papers.

>Office Of The Flag Officer
>East Africa
>Navel Headquarters
>Kilindini
>6th May, 1944

Memorandum No. EA. 01

Instructions For Search Of German Submarine Ashore Off Bender Beila

H.M.S "Fishguard" and "Prudent" are to sail for Bender Beila after embarking necessary personnel and material to carry out thorough search of German submarine run ashore off Bender Beila, rough position 09 degrees 35 minutes North and 48 minutes 30 seconds East.

The expedition is to be under the command of Commanding Officer, H.M.S. "Fishguard" who is to coordinate all work on the submarine by the specialist officers whose various activities are to be guided by paragraph 2 of my memorandum EA. 951/1 of 5th May 1944.

The object of the expedition is:-

i. To obtain all information possible as to German submarine practice, operations, ciphers etc. as indicated in paragraph 4 of the above mentioned Memorandum.

ii. Salvage of submarine if this appears possible, or

if salvage will entail a lengthy period of work, the possibility of towing her to a more sheltered position where salvage work could be more easily carried out, is to be considered.

No steps to carry out (ii) are to be taken without first referring to the Flag Officer, East Africa for decision, giving a full account of the situation and what is intended.

The Commanding Officer, H.M.S. "Fishguard" is to arrange that all precautions are taken to prevent injury to personnel by booby traps, or the firing of demolition charges. Information on this matter is given in Appendix 1 attached. An officer is to be detailed to co-ordinate all work on board the submarine and to ensure that the proper precautions have been taken before compartments or machinery are opened up.

There are six unexploded depth charges, due to shallow water, in the vicinity and ships are to be careful to anchor well clear of the line of approach to the submarine, on which track they are most likely to be. You will be informed as to rough position of these depth charges when known.

"Prudent" should be used with divers to search the position where the ship was blown up and back down the track if possible, to try and recover any documents and instruments etc. which may have been thrown overboard before scuttling.

The possibility of attack by enemy submarine must be borne in mind and all precautions taken. Air cover has been asked for.

You are to contact Army authorities at Bender Beila on arrival and make arrangements for embarkation of specialist officers who are being sent by air and land to assist in the work. All arrangements for hiring of local boats or dhows to be done through the Army.

A daily report on progress of work and future intentions or requirements is to be signalled to the Flag Officer, East Africa.

Subject to the precautions and responsibilities indicated above, the Commanding Officer, H.M.S. "Fishguard" is to be largely guided by the specialist officers as to what work is to be carried out in order to obtain the maximum success in the objects of this expedition.

Rear Admiral.

The Commanding Officer, H.M.S. "Fishguard"　(15)
The Commanding Officer, H.M.S. "Prudent"　　(5)
(The Admiral Superintendant, Kilindini)　　　　(5)

—

Appendix 1 – To The Flag Officer, East Africa's Memorandum No. EA01, Dated 6th May.

C.A.F.O. 1477 – **Scuttling Charges in German U-Boats**

(N.I.D. 03166/43 – 15 Jul. 1943)

The following unverified information has been received of the scuttling charges fitted in German U-Boats :-

2. Scuttling charges are of 10kg. and are always in position when the U-Boat is operating in enemy coastal waters (i.e. off the British or U.S. coasts).

3. These charges are fitted :-
a. In the After Machinery compartment, adjacent to one of the two H.P. air compressors, probably between it and the ship's side, on the outboard flange of the cooling water inlet pipe.
b. At the bottom of the periscope well.
c. In the bow torpedo compartment against the flange which connects the domed end of the pressure hull with the main.

Appendix Five

Report On U-boat (*U-852*)

The text below is copied from a document found amongst Stanley Butler's papers.

> H.M.S. "Raider"
> 6th May, 1944

REPORT ON U-BOAT (*U-852*)

Length:	About 250 feet.
Displacement:	Between 1,000 and 1,400 tons.
Beams:	24 to 26 feet.
Position:	U-Boat was lying on her port side with a list of about 30 degrees, in about 3 ½ to 4 fathoms. Bow and stern were blown off. (38 degree list) Amidships was intact, although flooded.
Hull:	The hull construction appeared to be on similar lines to our "H" Class boat. Although boat was listing to about 30 degrees, there was no sign of bilge keel.
Armament:	One 4.1 inch gun forward of the conning tower. The gun could be laid and trained from either side. Elevation not above 20 degrees. Range dials are in H.M.S. "Parrett". Arc of firing about Red 160 degrees to Green 160 degrees. One 37mm gun aft of conning tower. Five shells in clip. Action similar to our Bofore. Open cartwheel sight with "V" sight. A

small cartwheel sight is held in H.M.S. "Parrett".
Two twin 0.79 inch mountings on after end of conning tower. Clipped ammunition held in "Parrett". Guns acting on similar action to our Oerlikons. Cocking gear consists of link gear – pull a handle and the gun is cocked. Handle comes about 18 inches to rear.
A mounting with no gun is fitted abaft the forward gun on the casting. Ammunition was supplied up the conning tower hatch and down shuts to the forward gun.
Anti Aircraft guns had ready use hatches near the guns.

Torpedoes: 4 forward tubes.
2 after tubes.
8 upper deck torpedo stowage positions between the casting and the hull – 4 each side. These are horizontal and are about 1 foot apart, end to end. Method of shipping uncertain.
After body of torpedo seen in upper tube, starboard side, forward.
Possibility of head of torpedo in starboard lower tube. Air vessel on the beach. Port tubes not inspected.

D/F: A single D/F aerial was situated starboard side, forward of the bridge – housed position inside the conning tower.

W/T: Nothing seen.

Radar: Aerial was housed in casing port

	side of the conning tower. It could be raised and lowered from the control position. Training appears to have been fitted. Aerial was split dipole type – 8 split dipoles, 17 centimetres in length, set 2 centimetres apart. Four of them had screens or reflectors behind them.
Glider:	Stowage for glider was on after end of the conning tower. Two vertical circular bins held the glider – starboard side, the body. Port side, the wings, rudder and tail planes. Stowage was in-between the guides.
	A smaller hatch contained the tow wire – about 150 fathoms of 5/8 inch special flexible steel wire. An insulator fitted on the outboard end. A compressed air motor was fitted for winding in the wire. Abaft the storage position there was a platform for the pilots taking off position.
	The glider is in H.M.S. "Parrett".
Lower Conning Tower:	The position contained a great deal of gear, chiefly electrical. A Torpedo Deflection Calculator (fruit machine) was fitted.
	An electrical control panel with 9 voice pipes above it was fitted port side forward, with a gyro repeat on its starboard side, on the centre line. Starboard side forward contained electrical switches and junction boxes. On the starboard side aft there was a

large glass gauge about 3 feet in length. Periscopes came through this compartment. Wells on deck gave the impression that the periscopes were operated and used from this position, although the bottom of the periscopes could not be felt in the wells – under water. Two wire drums were visible, but operating was impossible.

Lieutenant – Commander in Command.

Printed in Great Britain
by Amazon